Freeing oneself from spiritual CONFORMISM

michel chiambretto

Discovery Publisher

Original Title: *Le troisième pas*, 2003, Chariot d'Or.
Second Edition, edited and augmented,
2021, ©Discovery, Michel Chiambretto

For the English edition:
2022, ©Discovery, Michel Chiambretto

Author: Michel Chiambretto
Translation: Vladimir Markov

616 Corporate Way
Valley Cottage, New York
www.discoverypublisher.com
editors@discoverypublisher.com
Fièrement pas sur Facebook ou Twitter

New York • Paris • Dublin • Tokyo • Hong Kong

Table of Contents

Freeing oneself from spiritual CONFORMISM

michel **chiambretto**

"[…] If the fringe of intuition surrounding his intelligence is capable of expanding sufficiently to envelop its object, that is the mystic life. The dynamic religion which thus springs into being is the very opposite of the static religion born of the myth-making function, in the same way as the open society is the opposite of the closed society."[1]

Henri Bergson

1. Henri Bergson, *The two sources of morality and religion*, University of Notre Dame Press, 1977, p. 268.

My thanks to Claudine, Marie, Paul, Thomas, Didier, Vlad and also to H.M. Chan Buddhist monk, Masters W.X.J. and W.S.W. of the Chinese internal tradition, Prior Don M. Roman Catholic, L.B.-M. Yoga Master, A.F. Master of the Occult, the F.: H.A., S.B., C.C., G.M., and Xue Yuan Kong Jin.

Important disclaimer

FOREWORD

In both past and present, there have always been two types of spirituality.[1] One offered to anybody, with a societal purpose, defining bans and taboos through dogmas, all the while presenting marvelous imagery and promising a well-being within reach, now or in the future, for those who follow the institution. And another type, more discreet, which, in contrast with the previous one, has for objective the accomplishment of Man and offers only a long work on oneself to achieve an expansion of the field of consciousness toward the Divine, the All, the One, the Tao, or whatever one wants to call it.

This is obvious! You will say like most people. But contrary to what you may think, the difference between these two aspects is often hidden under deceptive guises.

Of course, this does not concern you, you think you are able to discern the true from the false, the spiritual direction from the societal one, and this may actually be the case. However, I suggest that you read this book to the end, even if you feel disturbed by certain remarks or are shocked by examples that call into question your current certainties.

But believe me, what we will be addressing is not built on gratuitous assertions, but on real knowledge of authentic traditions practiced for tens of years by Seekers of all backgrounds, members of various schools, religious and initiatory, from both the West and the Far East. These traditions should not be confused with the various methods offered to a select public, or to the public at large,

1. Bergson, philosopher of consciousness, divides religion into: static religion and dynamic religion. The former has a societal function, while the latter has for objective the accomplishment of Man. Henri Bergson, *The two sources of morality and religion,* University of Notre Dame Press, 1977.

these are discreet practices that do not highlight the individual, do not make for party conversation, do not help in achieving a status — a personal or a societal dream, in other words, a new "mask."[1]

As with any tradition stemming from the Primordial Tradition[2], these are initiations which, free of any smoke and mirrors, allow after a long work on oneself, not to access the defined — a virtuous society, happiness with a capital H, a predefined spirituality — but a dimension that your mind cannot anticipate.

To help you in your future quest, the one that will allow you to find a genuine guide, I propose you in a first time to remove some of the illusions that can limit your reflective analysis.

A reflective analysis that can only be based on the conditioning you received since childhood through religious, societal and scholarly education, and more insidiously, the one delivered by the "Knowledgeables"[3] from the media, declared specialists of all spiritual paths.

What do you say? This is not your case. Well, we will verify this in the following pages, and if you feel upset, consider this feeling as something positive. Because, as you certainly know, freeing oneself of a conditioning requires the use of emotion and repetition; therefore, the more unbearable the rejection, the more you will advance on your new Path.

This can only be done with time, and thanks to what this book will leave inside you, unconsciously your perspective will change. Your mind will keep the memory of what initially appeared as an aberration, or a rambling, and progressively the promises offered by seductive, reassuring and empowering spirituality will make you smile softly, and for some, maybe also revolt you.

1. Mask, or Persona, according to C.G. Jung, denotes the part of the personality that organizes the relation between the individual and society.

2. Primordial Tradition: the one transmitted since the dawn of time, universal because of the essential nature of man.

3. Knowledgeable: "man of knowledge," where knowledge is of the realm of the intellect, in contrast with cognition, which is of the domain of experience.

Indeed, there are other seekers just like you, who wish, who want to go beyond themselves, who feel a need, a necessity to transcend, not to gain something "more" but really to dissolve in the ineffable. I beg your pardon? That last part confounds you? Do not be surprised, we have just started on the proposed path.

Let us begin by immersing ourselves in the different stages of any spiritual evolution, with the aim to define, as a first step, your state of consciousness.

THE COMMON MAN

Any person thinks he is the product of his inherent nature. The implication is that his personality has been formed by a natural impulse and in consequence his individuality has been able to bloom.

However, what follows could potentially go against this assertion. We know that any questioning of one's self-image is difficult, to say the least, even impossible. This is due to the fact that the self-image — *which is associated with the Self* — is often nothing other than the reflection of the established societal norms and, like any introspective analysis, uses Reason[1], which, molded by these same norms, cannot escape the conditioning imposed since childhood.

To open a first breach, we will look in more detail at the molding of the individual suffered by citizens of any country. This can also be called "the shaping of the common man."

The common man is a product of:

- Parents, family, education.
- Teachers, professors, his formal education.
- Priests, imams, rabbis, atheists, his "religion."
- Leaders, politics, legislation, intellectuals, coworkers, media, his society.

Most of the time he is not aware of it. Happy and satisfied, he himself participates in the molding of his children and loved ones, which he considers as essential.

Absurd and ridiculous?

---

1. Reason: the entirety of the intellectual faculties allowing to discern true from false, good from bad, and organizing one's relation with reality.

Well, let us observe the life of a random person.

The example that follows, with a few adjustments, appears to be universal in both past and present.

The child is born.

From that moment on, a relentless logic will "shape" the child, condition it and make it a perfect cog of an existing whole. The child must not only fit the whole, and thus correspond to the definition of an integrable element, but must also participate in the collective effort — *the common objective is very rarely expressed, because it is often idealized in political expression.*

One might think that, with this idea of integration, the child would already be able to understand that he is nothing but a microcosm inside the macrocosm of society, which was the basic ideology of communist countries. However this is antithetic to our contemporary society, which believes in individualism.

However, this did not change anything in reality, because any political indoctrination cannot but be opposed to any blossoming of the individual, and in consequence to any personal evolution.

It is important to look at this "relentless" logic in more detail.

From early childhood, the common man will be imposed a cliché reference of his future life. That is, the Ideal man who, of course, corresponds entirely to what his relatives have themselves received, all with the leitmotif:

"You must become an adult, my child!"

According to this predefined objective, the qualities required to be accepted inside the community are cultivated within the child:

- A man must be honest, he must respect the property of others.
- A man should not hurt another man, except if his country asks him to — *a paradox that should raise questions.*
- A man must love and respect his parents, his family, his teachers, his leaders, his...; the social hierarchy.

- A man must be taught according to the criteria of the education system of the country where he resides.
- A man must be a conscientious worker.
- A man must respect religious precepts — *or not, the political or philosophical doctrines substituting for said religion.*
- A man should not question the social references of the society he lives in — *with the exception of the revolutionary or communal substitutes, which are also dogmatic.*
- A man, etc.

These rules of life and thinking, initiated by the parents, will be further applied by the public — *or private* — education, or maybe the religious one. At the school, in the college, even in the university, the same principles will be taught, as well as the training allowing him to have a purpose in the macrocosm of society.

To complete this task successfully, all the principles of deep brain conditioning will be used — same as with any brainwashing:

- *Tireless repetition of the same topics;*
- *Emotional dimension; family, society, opposite sex;*
- *Multiple rewards or various threats and punishments;*
- *In addition, the "animal mimicry" is activated.*

In this way, he can become a worker ant, a manager ant, a fighter ant, a thinker ant, a knowledgeable ant, more rarely a leader ant, and in some exceptional cases, a Queen ant. The latter, often daughters of Queens, will be nourished differently. Right from their earliest childhood, their education will be different, especially before the nuptial flight, conducted in elite schools that will give them the required wings.

Everything is done and organized for the child, and later the adolescent, in such a way that he orients his life toward the upcoming integration in the macrocosm of society.

The child could, at some point, ask the following question:

"Why? Why spend the best time of my life, all my youth, all day long, in this collective education intended to make me useful and productive?"

But he will not ask it, because the answer has already been provided — it is his duty and if he does not do it, he will not conform to the image that he can be proud of, in his eyes and in the eyes of his loved ones.

This is the indoctrinated definition of happiness; which will later provoke the "middle-age crisis" when the concerned becomes aware of his aberrant way of life.

Additionally, there cannot be any doubt, everything around him confirms that this is the only way to obtain what everyone desires, that is to say:

– To be recognized socially,
– To be loved by his relatives,
– To be desired by the opposite sex,
– To be calm, without fear of the future, of the unknown.

This last point is omnipresent in the modern context, where people are worried about their future, where man lives in a permanent anxiety — *a feeling that undoubtedly helps to better control society.*

From the moment he starts working, his main objective is to accumulate enough stuff so he can live "without needs." And the main concern is to do everything possible to cope with tomorrow and with old age, even if this means depriving oneself during one's entire life.

The level of conditioning is impressive.

Man abstains from living fully his youth so as to receive the necessary education allowing him to… abstain himself from living fully his adult life so as to accumulate material goods that will allow him to… eventually live fully the few remaining years of his life, if he is still alive, if his health allows it, if he has the energy for it — *and if he manages to decondition himself…*

An intentionally negative perspective, but maybe not entirely wrong.

The established hierarchical structure will only reinforce this "system" by basing everything on the obtained diploma. It will allow or not the individual to claim this or that job and to thus acquire the corresponding social status. The social status becomes for him the reflection of his Being, or at least this is what he thinks.

> *Regarding self-image, C.G. Jung said: "Society expects, and indeed must expect every individual to play the part assigned to him as perfectly as possible [...] must at all times and in all circumstances play the role of persona in a flawless manner [...] hence the construction of an artificial personality becomes an unavoidable necessity.*[1] "

This "shaping" has become universal to such an extent that today it can be found even in domains whose initial role was to produce a certain awakening of the mind.

We can mention here, among others, the Initiatory Arts, the so-called schools of Awakening, the trendy spirituality and the philosophy courses[2], where the "Knowledgeables," as well as the teachers and the institutions, go through the sieve of intellectualism, of dualism, thus entirely excluding the experiential.

This confusion of categories only reinforces the initial conditioning and in turn increases the opacity of the veil covering the sensitive perception of man — *confusion from which genuine "Seekers"*[3] *are excluded.*

---

1. C.G. Jung, *Two essays on analytical psychology*, Collected Works, Vol. 7, Princeton University Press, 1967, pp. 192-193.

2. We mean here the ancient Traditions whose objective was to "awaken" the Spirit of the disciple through the use of initiatory tools, for example: Alchemy, Yoga, meditation, pranayama, philosophical contemplation, Zen, Yi King, Taoism, Tantric Buddhism, Freemasonry, Way — Do — of the martial arts, etc.

3. Seeker: "a man in quest," a path that is in the realm of the experiential.

The confusion is such that it is often forgotten that some of to-day's "sports" and "well-being activities" were initiatory Traditions when they were transmitted differently. This is to say, not with the aim of improving one's physical and mental condition, but rather developing one's field of consciousness.

And to complete the whole, rewards of all sorts are provided: honors, distinctions, titles, trophies, awards, and all kinds of accolades; in other words, the frame of reference for societal appraisal — *without forgetting the financial aspect, which does not surprise anyone anymore in this world of globalization.*

This principle is applied from the earliest days of schooling, when children are made to compete through grades, the whole assorted with various rewards and punishments. It continues all life long with a whole set of more or less gratifying benchmarks that follow the gradation of the community apparatus.

Some examples are "Club service" associations that only accept in their ranks the privileged, creating by this choice a new distinction of a pseudo-elite. To maintain the hierarchy of these clubs, members are co-opted based on their "societal value". Membership in a particular association defines the status of the member, and is sometimes highlighted by wearing a pin — *we are not that far away from the Hindu caste system.*

This last example, which can be found in some form in every society, shows that man, irrespective of his age, remains susceptible to smoke and mirrors. Proof, if any is needed, that spiritual evolution does not depend on age, intellectual quotient, education, or social standing.

It is often forgotten that the person with the highest IQ can be the most dim-witted one in other fields, such as self-knowledge — "intra-personal intelligence," the "sensitive." Which is confirmed by H. E. Gardner, professor in cognition, psychology and neurology: "There are savants who perform great feats of calculation even though they are tragically deficient in most other areas."[1]

---

1. Howard Earl Gardner, *Multiple intelligences, new horizons*, Basic Books, 2006, p. 12.

This addiction to status seeking is so prevalent in our societies that it follows the individual to his grave. Indeed, the tributes to the dead where medals, titles, distinctions and various praises flourish are plentiful — man remains in his illusion in all circumstances. Such "testimonials" are obviously based more around the existential references of the living than on the spiritual accompaniment of the deceased — *maybe that is why Leonardo da Vinci chose to be accompanied by sixty beggars during his burial.*

One could think then, quite logically, that man has the possibility of reconnecting with his "Essential being" through his relationship with religion. But here again, everything is definition, everything is conditioning, at least at the first level, that of the "static religion."

> *Bergson, philosopher of consciousness, distinguishes between static and dynamic religion. The static one is the social aspect of religion, serving to maintain society's cohesion. Conversely, the dynamic religion has as its objective the accomplishment of Man.*[1]

> *This same confusion was highlighted by René Guénon, who stated that Islam presents primitive Christianity as "Tariqa" — an initiatory path —, and not as "Sharia" — social legislation —, thus demonstrating the evolution of an initiatory message toward a moral path understandable by all and so intended for the greatest number of people.*[2]

> *An evolution that can be considered as generic to the contemporary religious, esoteric and initiatory domains.*

In our Judeo-Christian society, it all began with the Tablets of Law. Ten rules to strictly abide by, so as not to risk the wrath of a punishing God.

---

1. Henri Bergson, *The two sources of morality and religion,* University of Notre Dame Press, 1977.

2. Jean Marc Vivenza, *Le dictionnaire de René Guénon,* Le Mercure Dauphinois, 2002.

The ten commandments of the Mosaic law — which consisted of 613 laws — called the Decalogue, deka logoi — ten words —, whose source comes either from the Egyptians — 1000 years before the Decalogue, or the Babylonians — the Code of Hammurabi, 200 years before.

It is worth mentioning that Buddha himself, facing the growing number of people who wanted to follow his teaching, made the monks recite 10 vows — 8 for the laymen — the first few of which remind the Decalogue, namely:

- *Do not kill,*

- *Do not steal,*

- *Do not seduce the wife of another.*

Precepts which, despite being apparently obvious, seem to be indispensable to man in all latitudes.

Over time, this was completed by establishing what is authorized and what is not in the form of dogmatic definitions of "Good" and "Bad." Moreover, same as the "father" in the family unit, the "Divine" is omnipresent to monitor every act and thought — *the objective, in both past and present, is to control the animal that is in every man.*

And so, the man shaped by society finds, once again, the outlines of his "mold."

Everything is kept in boxes. You open the box of "Good" and you find a set of predefined topics. As a logical consequence, as soon as you tackle a new topic, you have to put it in this box or in the other one, that of "Bad." When in doubt, you will analyze it according to the instilled parameters, which will allow you to find the appropriate box. Also, you will have been taught beforehand that it is not possible to put it in two boxes at the same time or in a third one.

We see here a possible interpretation of the metaphor of Adam and Eve's exit from Paradise, to wit the image of a child's arrival in this world. That is to say, the immaculate child who, at its birth, takes on its animal nature, followed by the sexual one, and without forgetting the fruit of the tree of knowledge of good and evil — the binary —, its Reason.

It is clear that we are far removed from the sensitive relation that should exist between the subject and the "object."[1] We remain in the object definition.

The religious education, like the secular one, is made complete by the allure of the reward. If you do "Good," you are in fact a man of quality and the paradise is open to you. The paradise where man is happy and lives without working, because everything is given to him, where there is no hate, no aggression, no sickness, no poverty, no misfortune, no old age, no death; in other words, the opposite of life. However, if you do "Evil," the hell awaits you and you will suffer eternally the torments of life.

Obviously, the preceding description is a limited view of religion, but we are only at its first level, the "static"[2] one. It is this aspect that is often rejected by atheists, but the latter are equally dependent on the social conditioning received, with some theosophical and philosophical variations.

The didactic conditioning is complete. Scholastic education has done its work in both the social and religious fields, which are in complete synergy.

And indeed:

- A whole set of principles of societal life have been instilled in the subject.
- He has been taught to "spontaneously" adopt predefined behaviors, according to the situation.
- The foundations of analytical and logical reasoning have been inculcated, based on a binary approach to everything.

The realm of the Spirit[3] disappears just as much in the Arts, of-

1. Object: anything, animate or inanimate, that affects the senses.

2. Term borrowed from Bergson.

3. Spirit, spiritus (capital S in the text): "the corporeal/incorporeal substance" that connects man to God, to the Tao, to the universe, depending on everyone — not to be confused with the Soul. Also, not to be confused with "mind": commonly used to encompass the principles of the psychic life, the intellectual and emotional faculties, and sometimes the way of being.
Soul: transcendent principle of man, but also "pure individualized conscious-

ten reduced to limited methods and approached in an intellectual manner like the sciences. The latter are emphasized to prove the superiority of man over the animal — *which is confirmed by the religions.* Sciences called exact because demonstrated through analysis, logic, discursive analysis.

> *Konrad Lorenz, biologist and zoologist, states on this topic: "All too willingly man sees himself as the center of the universe, as something not belonging to the rest of nature but standing apart as a different and higher being. Many people cling to this error...*[1]*"*

And when the spiritual dimension is addressed, we are told that it is a different category which completely escapes common understanding. This is true to such an extent that it was necessary, at a certain point, to define Jesus as the son of God, and thus God himself — *by vote during the Council of Nicea in 325* — and not as a Guide, as an accomplished man, or as a... — *and consequently, without opening the mind of man to the undefinable.*

Moreover, in this definition of "belief," it was necessary to bring a miraculous dimension to the inherited metaphors and this despite the quality of the messages transmitted by them — *when the voluntary or involuntary translation is not too erroneous.*

> *The use of allegories and metaphors is particularly useful for any transmission. Indeed, words have their limits, with definitions that vary in time, and this is without mentioning that "to translate is to betray." The meaning of a metaphor avoids such issues.*

Everything that cannot be explained scientifically is miraculous. And the miracle does not depend on man, only the Divine can create it. The miracle has thus become essential to popular belief — *the very basis of this doctrine: it is not possible for a "believer" to think that the resurrection of Christ did not happen, because without this miracle, the transmitted message would lose its strength.*

---

ness," "sensitive perception," (and not individuation, personality, persona); it can be the link of consciousness, "the corporeal substance" that leads to the "incorporeal," the "Soul/Spirit."

1. Konrad Lorenz, *On Aggression*, Routledge, 2002, p. 213.

Except for the Cathar "heresy" which saw everything as a symbol.

For example, the resurrection is the rebirth in the Divine Spirit, the multiplication of the loaves corresponds to the "spiritual nourishment" given to the growing number of followers, the blind is the one who does not see the value of God — confirmed by "They have eyes, but they do not see" Jeremiah 5:21, etc.

This notion of miracle, very close to superstition, is also part of the conditioning received — *attractive "rattles" for the layman.*

The difference with the inner Impetus is at this level. The inner Impetus does not require proof, performances, miracles.

It is.

It is part of the Spirit.

This obviously does not mean that the "miracle," the "inexplainable," rationally does not exist.

Therefore, as a consequence of this education, of this "molding," what becomes of man?

Firstly, it seems obvious that he cannot but be cut off from his inner nature, from his "Essential being," which some call the "Other."

This "Other" is replaced by an amalgam of familial, social and religious components. And this "mask" covering his true nature is so integral to the individual that he is unable to dissociate himself from it. He thinks that his Being is the mask; a nice illusion!

To quote C.G. Jung: "[...] a kind of mask, designed, on the one hand, to make a definite impression upon others and, on the other, to conceal the true nature of the individual."[1]

I am: last name, first name, from such and such family, with such and such education, with such and such family situation, holder of such and such diploma, with such and such profession, owner of such and such property — *the whole placing me on the social scale* — having received such and such religious education, whether accepted or not.

1. C.G. Jung, *Two essays on analytical psychology*, Collected Works, Vol. 7, Princeton University Press, 1967, p. 192.

According to these criteria, the subject has unknowingly shaped his societal mask and especially the false image that he has of himself; and the others have helped him to perfect it because, by the same conditioned analysis, their eyes and their attitudes confirm it.

On the sensitive level, a part of his true nature has been preserved, that which concerns the love for his loved ones and, in some rare exceptional cases, the empathy for the suffering of others.

This part is linked to the Spirit, but is also often the object of the mental imbalance of the subject; which, by the way, is treated by bringing the observed irregularities back to the desirable state — *the role of the shrinks.*

The common man is finished.

This reminds Arthur Rimbaud, who, speaking of himself in 1871, wrote in his letter to George Izambard: "I is an Other."

And most people do not ask fundamental questions or very few. Indeed, logically enough, "What would be the point anyway?," "Why do it?," "What is the point?" Life is about the material. It is complex enough and there are plenty of problems to solve. Which is undoubtedly true and a spiritual quest can be considered a luxury.

Is this luxury only for the shirtless or for those sufficiently affluent? Do these two extremes meet? Luxury that monks allow themselves by retreating into monasteries, cut off from the world, thus forgetting the material constraints of everyday life and above all escaping the ambient mimicry.

The life of the common man will pass without the desire to reconnect with his Spirit. Blocked and rejected, his Spirit will only be able to express itself partially and on rare occasions. It will be called intuition, gift, premonition, visions, supra-sensorial perceptions, sixth sense. His spirituality will be limited to the respect for whatever has been inculcated to him since childhood, consciously or unconsciously.

Others, in their desire to awaken to new and better performing spirituality once adults, will convert to Eastern or Far Eastern traditions[1]. But in reality nothing will change, the spiritual expression will happen through regular rites whose transcendental function has always been hidden, if not forgotten; most of the time what guides this impulse for change is the interest for temporary non-conscious performances.

And, as a logical consequence, there will be a common confusion between the disinterested approach to Faith[2] and the superstition with the objective of gain; hence the existing confusion between religion and belief.

> It is always useful to remind that etymologically Religion can mean: Relegere "rereading the texts," but also and mainly Religare (to) "link" and Religio "scrupulous attention; conscience."

From this confusion will emerge acts with undetermined motives:

- Baptism of the child mainly to respect the tradition — *forgetting that the theoretical objective is to introduce the baby in the Christian community by purifying it from the original sin.*
- "Religious" marriage, "because this is how it is done" — *and also and especially because the memory of the fairytales of princes and princesses getting married is at the level of the long memory.*
- Funerals in accordance with the customary form — *and to honor the dead.*
- Prayers, devotions, meditations, pilgrimages with a personal objective of well-being — *and not to "merge into the Divine."*

For most people, the conditioning received will remain active during their entire lives.

---

1. No criticism intended for these traditions, which also have their hidden "dynamic" side.

2. By Faith the author means "an inner call toward an ineffable absolute beyond any definition."

On purpose, we omitted to describe:

- The idolatrous drift of men toward their fellow men. Idolatry, initially cultivated by religious education and directed toward the powerful, the affluent, those in the media, the leaders, the Chosen.
- The paradox between the quality of the ideas transmitted by a few and the mediocrity of the deeds done by everyone.
- The intolerance, the racism, the xenophobia, the chauvinism, the ambient sectarianism,
- The exploitation of the weak,
- The natural egocentrism,
- The cruelty toward other species,
- And many other things…

There is much more to say. Too much.

The picture is complete.

We are aware that this is a caricature and therefore excessive — *although…*

When reading logion 29 of the Gospel of Thomas[1], *one could think that Jesus' opinion on the nature of man is not the most optimistic, to quote:*

"Jesus said: "If the flesh came into being because of the spirit, it is a wonder. But if the spirit (came into being) because of the body, it is a wonder of wonders. Yet I marvel at how this great wealth has taken up residence in this poverty."

It is true that in the preceding logion Jesus says: "I stood in the midst of the world, and I appeared to them in the flesh. I found them all drunk; I found none of them thirsting, and my soul was afflicted for the sons of men;"

Kabir, the Hindu-Islamic poet, echoes the words of Jesus in his observation on the human condition, fifteen centuries later:

---

1. Gospel of Thomas, quotes from multiple sources, see bibliography.

"All are intoxicated with the wine of maya; no one is awake and aware."[1]

Of course, it is obvious that everything we described allows people to coexist in the best way possible.

This "molding" has transformed "the wild animal" into "a domesticated one." Tamed by conditioning, domesticated by religious and legislative threats. Which is indispensable considering that, as with any trained animal, the ferocious side of man can flare up at any moment, when the threat of the stick disappears.

The result is that this "humanized" animal has lost, over time, any connection to the "Other," its essential Being. For most people this is not an issue at all because, as described, the nature of this presence is not known — *at least at the level of their Reason*. However, for some, the repressed intuitive perception of this loss is the cause of a profound ill-being.

An ill-being similar to embers that only need to be rekindled...

---

1. Kabir, quotes from multiple sources, see bibliography.

FIRST STEP
THE EXISTENTIAL
QUESTIONING

The first step of any spiritual evolution consists not in a state of serenity, nor in aiming at such a state of well-being, so dear to the "merchants of Happiness," but in the perception of an "ill-being" felt deep inside oneself. An "ill-being" that leads the individual to begin his first quest.

This can be one of the interpretations of logion 16 of the Gospel of Thomas:

"But they do not know that I have come to bring the world discord, fire, sword, war."

Same as Matthew 10:34 "Think not that I am come to send peace on earth: I came not to send peace, but a sword."

Both quotes refer to the inner battle.

An undertaking that is surprising to most people, even aberrant; they understand neither its meaning, nor the point of it. In their eyes, this type of behavior cannot be justified, because for them, since there is nothing to be found, there is nothing to look for. For others, it is useless because everything has already been said and written.

This passive state is certainly the result of having received, since childhood, precise answers to questions never asked; which undoubtedly results in the abrogation of any future questioning.

So as to avoid this behavioral platitude, it seems necessary to ask ourselves the following question:

"What are the reasons that may lead some people to step out of their "mental comfort zone"? — *"mental comfort zone," because it delimits everything, as much on the social level as on the religious one, and even the philosophical one.*

Of course, the answers may vary, but for the majority of these exceptions, a "sensitive dissonance" manifests itself between the teaching received and their own field of consciousness — *a question of deep inner nature.* And, as a consequence of this "misalignment," a certain "inner awakening" appears which translates into a quest for truth — *a progression that seems obvious in hindsight, but which is experienced as a "profound ill-being" beforehand.*

In some other cases, the origin of this "awakening" may be external:

- *A psychic trauma causing a spiritual "opening."*
- *A particularly enriching encounter leading to a new approach,*
- *The work done in an initiatory school of quality.*
- *And sometimes the origin is "natural," the innate. The monks in their monasteries and the anchorites are obvious examples.*

It is at this point that appear, for the first time, the famous existential questions:

- "Who am I really?" or in other words: what is my essential nature?
- "Where do I come from?" or: what is the origin of my essential nature?
- "Where am I going?" or: what is the meaning of my life?

It must be pointed out that this craving is felt deep within oneself and that it should not be confused with the will of the "mask" — *that is to say, a search for status, for gains or for power — aspirations corresponding to the drift of the common man toward dead ends.*

These questions will elicit in the "apprentice Seekers" the most accessible approach today, which are the philosophico-religious references recognized by the general public.

They will then turn to essays, conferences, seminars dealing with ancient or modern philosophers, or they will concern themselves with authentic "religious schools" or those offering a spiritual awakening within everyone's reach. This will logically be followed by an exploration of psychoanalysis and psychology with the hope to understand their interiority.

Obviously, for all of them, the method of approach will be the one received initially, that is to say, the discursive one, of analysis and logical synthesis. It might be feared that, once again, this would only "thicken the layer"[1] that covers the minds of these "Seekers." This is partly true, but the extent of the field of exploration is such that, with time, rationalization becomes impossible.

This impossibility, first and foremost, comes from the fact that the initial certainties fall. The person appears more complex and this complexity takes many forms depending on the sources used. Religious texts present him under several facets, more or less embellished, with multiple degrees of comprehension — *that is to say, at the first level, the material, social, simple and basic aspect, but also another possible approach at the second level, through the analysis of parables with multiple interpretations.*

The relationship between man and his environment, man and the Universe, man and the Divine, is presented as more complex than the notion of enslavement initially instilled.

The ancient philosophers bring in principles and parameters that are much more subtle than the rigid laws of society — *or of dogmatic religion.*

Psychoanalysis exposes the different manifestations of the psyche and their mechanisms, which frustrates the confidence of the behavioral and existential mask.

Modern philosophy introduces the complexity of the ambient social behavior and can help grasp some part of the conditioning received.

1. The layer is the conditioning that covers the Essential Being, or in other words, the "Other" inside oneself.

And the more the investigation advances, the more the certainties of the "Seeker" fade away.

However, there is a major pitfall to avoid on the path of this beginning quest. Otherwise, the "apprentice Seeker" will go back to the initial forks in the road, while remaining convinced that he is moving forward in his search.

This first pitfall is the one that claims the most "victims." It consists in limiting one's search to a single group, thinking that it represents "The Truth." Truth made, once again, of limited definitions, which will quickly become bondage.

It is true that it is always attractive to discover "a new trendy tradition" — *even if it only shows its "static" face*. It is a change of scenery, sometimes rewarding because of the differentiation offered, and it provides the possibility to escape from one's societal "routine," or even, to an extent, from one's initial conditioning. Nevertheless, this "state of attraction" or "fascination" is to be avoided. Rather, it is necessary to shake oneself up and to look for what is "behind the façade offered to the greatest number of people."

It is important to know that the key teachings are always hidden, not only from the layman, but also from the "first degree" initiate — *this is true for all authentic traditions*. The holders of the "Primordial Tradition[1]," these "Masters from the shadows," do not appear on the front pages of the media and do not give public lectures — *which, for those in the know, can only be opposed to the transmitted messages*. They have kept for the oral transmission, that of "heart to heart,"[2] some fundamental points essential to the good understanding of the use of the provided tools.

This principle often shocks the layman. Which can be translated as:

---

1. A reminder: by Primordial Tradition the author understands the one transmitted since the dawn of time, universal because of the essential nature of man.

2. A "heart to heart" transmission is the one between a Master and a disciple that goes beyond words and gestures, and that appeals to the supra-sensory, to the "intention of the Heart" — *one of the translations of Logos*.

- "Why not offer to everyone, "free of charge," the possibility to access the entirety of the teaching?"
- And indeed:
- "Is this not the consequence of a sectarian will of these Masters?"

The answer is complicated.

But it can be said that only this type of transmission, from "heart to heart," allows to preserve the operational quality of the tools of the Tradition — *and especially, to initiate the awakening of the sensitive, supra-sensory dimension of the initiate.*

In addition, there are two other reasons for this principle.

- At a "certain level," the evolution of the field of consciousness allows the Seeker to possess "possibilities of supra-sensory influences" which must remain in the hands of men of quality so as to avoid any undesirable drift.
- On the other hand, as can be observed nowadays, without this principle the tools received would very quickly become nothing but products on the market, promising miraculous results, and will thus lose any virtue — *the financial aspect that is quite commonplace nowadays.*

These Masters from the shadows are filters responsible for the selection of people to be initiated — *which is true in all initiatory traditions "of quality."*

Jesus, who was compassion itself, said in his "hidden words" that "I speak my mysteries to those who are worthy of my mysteries. What your right hand does, let not your left hand know what it does."
—Gospel of Thomas 62

"Do not give what is holy to the dogs, lest they cast it on the dung heap." —Gospel of Thomas 93

Initiatory Christianity remains very opaque, even today, for the common man. But it is also true that the adaptations and interpretations of the canonical texts have only reinforced the phenomenon. This notion of secret is still very present in the Far East in Tantric

Buddhism, Chan, Taoism and in all internal arts — excluding the "products" offered to the public at large, of course.

"The ancients who showed their skill in practicing the Tao did so, not to enlighten the people, but rather to make them simple and ignorant." —Tao Te Ching 65.

Therefore, in order to avoid the pitfall of limiting one's search to a single group, it is necessary to open oneself up to all spiritual horizons with caution and discernment.

At least in the beginning, because over time, if the quest is "right," the difference between the intellectual understanding of spiritual topics and the sensitive approach resulting from the experiential realm becomes obvious.

On the one hand, one can find all the references of the subject matter treated, useful for the seduction of the layman. That is to say, the subject matter presented with the stereotypes expected by the "conditioned eye" of the layman, without forgetting the promises of results allowing to dream about one's future. And on the other hand, a developed sensitivity, through which one perceives the lived experience.

But for this, it is good to always remember the words of Lao-Tzu:

"True words are not pleasing. Pleasing words are not true." —Tao Te Ching 81

Through this opening of the mind, the Seeker will realize that the same subject can be interpreted in many different ways and that it is absurd to try to put it in a single box.

Any "definition" will thus become multiple and with this multiplicity reaching the infinite the first notion of unicity will appear to him.

This first destabilization will give rise to a desire to deepen the quest which, at this stage, will most often be motivated by the desire for egocentric fulfillment — *which will become undesirable, to say the least, later on.*

So, the Seeker will read works from various traditions and will approach other people who are also seeking. He will finally learn to listen to others attentively, without preconceived ideas, and will thus be able to realize that his prejudices were often the expression of his own limitations. However, as an inevitable consequence, the chaotic order that he will perceive will make him lose his old bearings, and this will be uncomfortable.

It is important to insist on this last point.

If the Seeker joins some group, even a quality one, he will find at the beginning a whole set of elements useful for his progression: method, tools, synergy with the others. But with time, as in any microsystem, the comfort will come back and with it the lack of mental motivation necessary to any quest. As a consequence, the risk of a new conditioning will appear.

Indeed, some groups and institutions have a whole range of "lures" that are very useful to attract the layman. But these lures, over time, can become traps from which only few manage to escape.

For example, the outfits of all kinds, the dialectic proper to every institution, the attitude linked to the ambient mimicry, the repeated self-aggrandizement, all progressively cover the new initiate with a new layer — *a layer that longstanding members continue to wear.* Without forgetting the rules, created to achieve a certain harmony between the members, but which become immutable references for many, thus structuring their minds.

> *This corresponds to most initiatory or religious institutions, in the West as well as in the East or the Far East, at least if one is careful enough to have a "detached" perspective.*

But let us remain positive, this part of the path can be very useful and enriching if one is able to avoid the pitfalls of the ambient system. Which, to be honest, is rare, to say the least, after a while.

The recommendation not to limit the search to a single institution is not the only pitfall to avoid during this phase. In fact, the traps are so numerous that it is difficult to be exhaustive. But what characterizes them is their perverse nature, because they elicit the preconditioned responses of our "conditioning" and so are frighteningly effective. Thus, one falls into the trap without realizing it and in reality pursues a quest that is just an illusion.

These "snares of illusion" are often presented under the name "Tools of Awakening" or in the form of "*effective* spirituality." Tempting promises, because they are based on the desire of the common man to achieve a "state" superior to his own, specifically to distinguish himself from the rest, from the ordinary men. In reality, though, these traps only transform the initial mask by giving it a new look and so increase the opacity of the Essential Being.

> *For the experienced Seeker, it is always surprising to see the impact that a uniform can have on the common man. An impact that is useful for law enforcement, as well as for religions — the static dimension. One example is the members of religious structures who must wear outfits formalizing their rank. Another is Buddhist speakers who appear in the media with a shaved head, a robe and a helpful smile. Without forgetting certain Westerners, "specialists" of Taoism, who appear on the covers of some publications wearing ancient Chinese outfits. Etc. It should be emphasized that in the monasteries, on the contrary, the objective of the monk's robe is to merge the individual with the collective of his brothers — in the same way that the tonsure is a symbol of the renunciation of worldly goods.*

It is not possible to talk about these "snares of illusion" without mentioning one of the most common mistakes, which is to confuse "a quest toward one's essential Being," "to awaken the Other inside oneself" with "cultivating oneself." A culture which, while interesting, will only strengthen the Ego of the Seeker over time.

This is certainly the most common and the most insidious pitfall because, as previously mentioned, it is the "Knowledgeables[1]" who

---

1. A reminder on the difference between "Knowledgeable" and "Cognizant": knowledge is of the realm of the intellect, while awareness stems from experience.

have created most works of reference. And it is often these same "Knowledgeables" who teach and obtain positions and titles in the various contemporary spiritual or initiatory schools, thus becoming unavoidable references themselves.

> *Chan Buddhism knows how to give examples allowing to understand the difference between "knowledge and cognition"; for example, with this type of question: "How do you explain pain to someone who has never felt it?"*
>
> *The difference is that "knowledge" is at the level of the intellect, while "cognizance" is of the experiential realm and therefore, at the level of the sensitive.*
>
> *Alexandra David-Neel called it "transcendent insight."*

Could these be intentional "lures" meant for the laymen?

Laymen do not appear surprised to see a total contradiction between humility, a precept common to all authentic Traditions, and the egocentric self-display of these "references" of spirituality.

Who has not seen a book with an "Enlightened one" — *or a "sage, philosopher, chosen one, spiritual representative, "religious" person, etc."* — shown on the front cover, donning a circumstantial smile, demonstratively blissful, without forgetting the various self-aggrandizing titles and laudatory references. This is quite common...

> *Not to be confused with some religious people who work for others while disregarding themselves, and this even while suffering physically and mentally.*

Indeed, the common man needs the outward aspect, the magnificence, the knowledge, the societal benchmarks, to admit the *"superiority"* of the other. A notion of superiority instilled during his initial conditioning and which is consequently the foundation of the judgments voiced — *while any accomplishment must go through the evolution of "values."*

Accordingly, it is necessary to constantly repeat that a purely cultural approach only touches the Reason, and that to touch the Spirit, one must remember to forget the theory so that the experience can allow the "Other" to express himself — *and this thanks to the tools of the Tradition transmitted — all authentic Traditions insist on this.* Bookish theories, acquired culture, multiple "knowledges," while useful in some cases to find the path to follow, must not become a burden afterwards.

Zhuang Zhou evokes this principle in the following question:

"Where can I find a man who has forgotten words so I can have a word with him?1"

Lao-Tzu affirms it:

"Those who know are not learned. Those who are learned do not know."

Or:

"The wise do not have great learning; those with great learning are not wise." —*Tao Te Ching 81*

Kabir confirms it in his verses:

"O scholar, you think you know it all from books, like a blind man who wants to describe an elephant!"

Same as Tauler, disciple of Meister Eckhart:

"Assume no airs of superior wisdom. Look in all simplicity into your own hearts..."2

Continuing with this list of insidious pitfalls, there is one that is more subtle; it concerns the confusion that can exist between belonging to a Tradition and the "fusion" to be achieved with the Tools of said Tradition. It is important to know that these tools require a particular know-how to become operational. Such knowledge is given only to a few carefully chosen initiates, at least in theory. Unfortunately, despite this rigorous selection, the Tools can have an effect opposite to what is intended or expected. This may seem surprising, but is actually not that rare. This is why it is essential to address this part of the path in more detail.

---

1. *The Complete Works of Zhuangzi*, Columbia University Press, 2013, p. 233.

2. *The sermons and conferences of John Tauler*, 1910, p. 280.

First of all, it should be made clear that the theory of the Tool received should not become the element that monopolizes the attention of the Seeker. In such a case, "using" the Tool will become more important than the "guiding intention" — *to avoid saying "the objective"* —, the Tool thus supplanting the Work. This confusion between Tool and Work is frequent, and it can be found in all initiatory paths, whether religious, symbolic or artistic.

As examples, we can look at the following "philosophico-religious"[1] teachings: Tantric Buddhism and Hinduism.

If luck, chance, karma, destiny, or whatever one wishes, is kind, the layman, after a long search, will be able to meet an authentic "Man who is on the path to Enlightenment."

In this regard, it is obvious that it is not desirable to think that the title is the quality. A lama can be the most blatant of impostors, just like a priest, a pastor or an Imam for that matter.

Consequently, the "lucky" layman will be able to follow the path indicated by this Guide — *but with caution and circumspection at first; indeed, does the subject have the quality, the necessary level of accomplishment to recognize a good guide?*

The others, the less "lucky" ones, much more numerous, will have to study these "fashionable thought trends" either by reading specialized books or by attending the conferences and seminars offered — *or nearly so…*

Accordingly, they will:

- Have to learn the complex history of the school(s); which is, of course, idealized,
- Be required to remember all Divinities, symbols, entities, as well as the theoretical principles and logic that underlie them,
- Need to know all texts of reference and associated commen-

---

1. Are Buddhism and Taoism religions? The answer can be "yes and no." No, if one considers that the word "religion" can be translated as "relegere," meaning "to reread." Yes, if it is translated as "religare," meaning "to link," in the sense of "linking oneself to." Always the same two aspects: static and dynamic.

taries, foundations of the doctrine, the rites, the names and
many other elements…
– Among other things…

This is an avalanche of information that the individual will have
to store by using only his Reason — *the time that the layman will
have to devote to integrate all this data is so long that it will take his
entire life.*

Again, he will be told of the miracles that have been accomplished, he will be promised Happiness and Enlightenment[1], the
qualities of reference — *wisdom, altruism, etc.* — and the end of
suffering.

Moreover, he will be threatened at the same time; this will be
the risk of being reincarnated in inferior lives — *"stick and carrot," paradise and hell.* And, most surprisingly, he will not draw any
parallels between the new precepts taught and the ones received
during his childhood.

> *You change the wrapping paper and the layman thinks that he has
> taken a step toward accomplishment, "Exoticism, orientalism, you
> intoxicate me!"*

It must be said that these traditions, extracted from societies
from different ages, have established their influence by deifying
their representatives. And Western converts participate in rites of
submission in front of children declared Tulkus — *"reincarnations"
of Lama* — so much so that the Dalai Lama himself had to, in front
of this negative image, say that it is essential to behave as an adult
in front of children — *yesterday's image should not be today's.*

> *Using your imagination, transpose the Tantric rite to the Chris-
> tian one. Imagine a Trappist monk — who certainly has nothing
> to envy to a Lama in terms of "internal work" — who would
> be greeted on one's knees. Who would be called "Unsurpass-*

---

1. Hui Neng, patriarch of Chan Buddhism in the 8th century: "The ignorant
person practices seeking future happiness, and does not practice the Way, and
says that to practice seeking future happiness *is* the Way." Hui Neng, *The Platform Sutra of the Sixth Patriarch,* Columbia University Press, 1967, p. 154.

able" — Lama — and children would be adulated as reincarna-
tions of the Trappist. What would you think of that?
This does not change the fact that, behind this façade, one can
find in Tantrism an initiatory tradition of great quality, with tools
whose effectiveness is indisputable — provided that you are shown
the proper use and progression, as always...

Regarding the so-called spiritual work, it will mainly consist in replicating the standard "format of the enlightened practitioner" — *both in terms of appearance and concept* — given by the teaching received. In consequence, the molded person, without realizing it, will play the role of the Awakened one or the Perfect one, thinking that he has been transcended by the theories instilled into him. But how can he move forward from this point when, once again, he is fooling himself about his state and his Being?

The state of Awakening, of Perfection, which corresponds to the "standard" of the doctrine, is a symbolic objective. Playing at being in the state will only add a new mask over the previous one, and this one will be definitive, because the path ends.

This is all the more to be avoided since the support of any spiritual path, of any personal quest, is self-acceptance. And this acceptance can only begin by knowing "oneself," one's shortcomings, imperfections, capabilities, qualities, and the social mask covering them.

This perception should progressively increase awareness of one's mask and what it covers, by accepting who one is, even if it does not correspond to the desired or desirable image for oneself or for others.

It is absolutely necessary to repeatedly remind ourselves that, like everyone else, we are conditioned and what we often think we are, personality, will, choices, desires, is only the result of a "social training," which overlays, very fortunately, our atavistic animal impulses. This humble and sincere approach to the self allows us, with time, to intuitively sense that there is something hidden deep within each one of us, an Essential Being[1] in contact with the Divine, the Universe, the Tao, with "something else that cannot be defined." This is confirmed by all traditions. This "Other" inside us, which is "our part of the divine," allows us to put down our mask and also to kill, or at least to domesticate, the sleeping animal. But we are not yet at this stage.

This awareness of the existence of the mask must gradually allow to see the contours of its influence. These contours go from visible to invisible, from appearance, behavior and intellect to the world of perception.

We believe we see, hear, smell, taste, touch, and we think we do it naturally, but using this method we can realize that we do it through the mask, which modifies or even transforms our sensitive dimension. The conditioning goes from perception to emotion and affects everything that is linked to them: love, hate, fear, compassion, empathy... We then discover that what we thought we felt was often nothing but an orchestrated reaction.

This is why some people turn to psychoanalysis. An interesting science, if working with fine practitioners, taught in a school that is not too indoctrinating. Therapy through analysis can be, as previously said, very useful to some people in difficulty, to detect and potentially heal their psychoses. But there is something that should not be forgotten:

– The therapist's function is that required by his patient, which is to remove the "ill-being" felt.

As a result, the practitioner finds himself obliged to "reinstall" the mask of the patient, so that the latter can reintegrate the social context with peace of mind. And so there is a difficult to define line between what is useful on the therapeutic level and what is undesirable on the spiritual one.

We exclude here the "indispensable" on the therapeutic level, which concerns serious behavioral issues.

The relationship between psychoanalysis and the Essential Being

1. Which the author calls "the Profound" in the text.

necessarily raises questions. The work of analysis can also be very, very long and lead to an egocentric attitude of little spiritual interest. The "via regia," the royal highway of the unconscious, which is the dream, according to psychoanalysis, should not be confused with a spiritual quest. This error can be found in the amalgamation of the unconscious, the psyche and the Essential Being.

The thirst for Knowledge leads many Seekers to the initiatory teachings. For example, the Freemasonry. A brotherhood whose work is based on the symbol, the Rite and the brotherhood. The interpretations of the symbol are multiple and vary according to the quality of the member. Thanks to this lack of definition, any sensitive experience can be transmitted without it being subjected to the ravages of time and a limited interpretation. Which suggests that man has been able to better communicate his knowledge through the symbol than through writing. The symbol can express the lived sensitive dimension and allows to approach it — *it should be emphasized that today the use of dictionaries of symbols is trivialized and because of that the principle itself disappears.*

Thanks to their effect on the unconscious, the Rites allow, depending on the quality of the recipient, to open unexpected fields of consciousness, on the condition that they are performed according to the Tradition.

> *There is often confusion between "being a good technician" of the ritual, of the breath, of the principles — which means painstakingly and conscientiously working the given techniques — and the stimulation of the Being — which leads to an exaltation of the Spirit, consequence of a "right," and not necessarily rigorous, work. In the first case, we are talking about an activity, in the second, an initiatory Art.*
> *A very frequent confusion.*

The brotherhood is the linchpin of the sensitive, a first step toward the love of the other[1], toward Unity. The work done is im-

---

1. "What is love if not the need to come out of one's self", Charles Baudelaire, *Mon Cœur mis à nu*, Éditions G. Grès et Cie, 1920, p. 114.

portant for the evolution of the brother. Work done by himself, making him ask the questions that he probably never would have asked. Work done by a brother, enriching, offering new unknown perspectives, and above all, done with humility; because often the most discreet brothers are those who have the most sincere — *and not egotistical* — quest.

A very idyllic vision, but unfortunately, as within any microcosm, the opposite also exists. We are not going to talk about the wheeler-dealers, whose only goal is profit and who tarnish all structures, including spiritual ones, but rather about the existing "molding" aspect.

Here again, we find the usual pitfalls.

First of all, during meetings — *reunions* — the incessant reminding of the Freemasonry ideal: tolerance, brotherhood, open-mindedness and spiritual accomplishment. Over time, the ceaseless repetition of the theoretical qualities leads the member to think that simply belonging to the institution is enough to create these qualities in him. And so he works intellectually on them, listens to the work of others on these topics and thinks that he "naturally" possesses them.

Of course, this is but a sweet dream, because all that happens is that a new format is created. The mask of the clone of the Freemason then appears, corresponding to the "stereotype image" of the institution. And to consolidate the whole, the ranks achieved inside this microcosm will only confirm the illusion. What is forgotten, though, is that only Reason has understood the process to follow so as to receive the recognition sought inside this microcosm.

At this moment, without noticing it, the member moves from the status of a Seeker to that of a careerist. Nothing surprising then to see that the institution becomes more and more important in his eyes, more than his own accomplishment. Again, we see the usual pitfall of any group — *the Tool supplanting the Work.*

This is not to disparage this institution, on the contrary — *it is only an example among many others.* The Tools offered — *Rites, symbols, brotherhood* — are of quality. They act on the perceptive so that afterward the speculative can understand the reasons of its evolution. They also act on the emotions of the brotherhood developed through the initiations and on the exaltation induced by the brotherhood. Excellent tools that promote the real accomplishment of the few exceptions who have not fallen into the traps.

Of course, we are looking at different aspects of the same pitfalls. But this reiteration is to serve as a "mirror" to your own journey, knowing that the wider the field of investigation is, the bigger the chances are that one of these numerous examples will hit close to home.

Indeed, any form of self-criticism is difficult, to say the least. Some will tell themselves that even though the institutions mentioned do present this shortcoming, theirs is different on many levels. Sure, but this remains improbable, especially if rather than looking at the differences that one wants to see, one looks at the similarities mentioned. To do this, it is enough to realize that the same dead-ends can be found even in the most pared-down schools.

As proof of this, let us end this chapter with Zen, unadorned school par excellence — *knowing that numerous schools exist in Japan*. Its main tool is seated meditation without thinking — *together with work on the Koan for the Rinzai school — exchanges between a Master and a disciple in which usual logic is out of place, the goal being to break pure Reason and reach the Spirit.*

This Japanese branch of Buddhism serves as a reference for this type of work and can only be respected. However, the same shortcomings can be found, namely:

- Numerous texts defining the typical model practitioner.
- The stereotypical way of thinking, which brings about the "definition" of Zen.
- The precisely defined posture, which becomes a straitjacket for the practitioner.
- The analysis of the multiple meanings of the Koan done by certain essayists, which limits, or even negates, its effect at the

level of the Spirit.

- The cultivated appearance — the attire, the shaved head, the apparent gravitas —, which models and externalizes the reference.
- The egotistic desire for recognition of some, the fights for influence of the institutions.
- The organization of traineeships and seminars for the general public in the West, which transforms this path of Awakening into a lucrative activity of little interest — *and this, even if a summary training in meditation is provided.*

Here again, from a school of great quality, man can create a pale ersatz — *a euphemism.*

The awareness of the Seeker of the works of illusion encountered is certainly the first step in any quest. Works of illusion which in reality are nothing but the renewal of the principles used in the initial conditioning, but presented in a different packaging, in a different way, in a different form.

This revival, or awakening, allows the Seeker, by analogy, to grasp the details of his own conditioning, how it was orchestrated and why. Henceforth, he knows that the real objective is not to answer his egocentric existential questions, nor to improve his culture, meaning Reason, but rather to connect with the Essential Being buried deep within him, which he still has to call "Other," because it is mysterious, not yet perceptible.

It is on this last point that he is not fooled. He knows that this is only the beginning of the path and that it is necessary to make the most of any opportunity to advance. He is vigilant, he knows that such opportunities pass at the speed of a galloping horse and that one must be ready to encounter Fate. His quest is relentless and inextinguishable, comparable to that of a thirsty man unable to find a source of water. The world around him now seems "foreign," cradled in the velvety comfort of sanitized thought, like a long calm river of little interest.

Conversely, his Spirit is boiling like a torrent.

SECOND STEP
THE PATH TOWARD
THE ESSENTIAL

One day, something obvious reveals itself to the Seeker. So obvious that he wonders why he could not perceive it earlier?

Recall that, during the previous stage, the Seeker learned to break free from all traps of illusion and to follow only the authentic Traditions and their "dynamic" aspect. For that, it was useful for him to learn not to reject this or that tradition, of this or that origin, because of its "packaging." This colorful packaging was unpleasant to his eyes, but he knew that the contents could still be of interest. And he also knew not to become intoxicated by any shimmer, again without rejecting the contents.

It is this state of mind that allowed him, over time, to move toward the essence of the Traditions encountered and to discover the similarity of the principles underpinning them. This similarity, this obviousness revealed, he perceived it when he had the privilege to be initiated to the "right" way of using the "Tools[1]" of the different authentic Traditions.

A small parenthesis regarding authenticity.
There are, as we have pointed out, in every tradition two lineages. One intended to bring "moral" to ordinary people. This moral is presented as having a supernatural origin, coming from an omnipotent and omniscient God entity, or from an Enlightened being who is venerated as a God, or from a Miracle worker. Conse-

---

1. By "Tools" we mean the "process" allowing to widen the field of consciousness — for example, prayer, meditation, contemplation, *pranayama* etc.

quently, it is perceived as inescapable, so as not to risk the anger of the supernatural forces, or hell, or reincarnation as a lesser being; always the stick — or the carrot.

A moral which, at its origin, has been put in place by "religious" elders to educate the society they were living in, to control the animal inside every man. And later imposed on the flock as an immutable doctrine — or almost, because with time...

Those in charge of this tradition are at the forefront. They have the appropriate image, the necessary charisma, and are at the top of the established pyramidal structure. It could be said that they are devoting themselves to be the shepherds of the flock; this is the exoteric Tradition — the static religion.

The second lineage is more discreet and sometimes secret. It has not only the profound knowledge of the Tools of the Tradition, but also continues to tirelessly work with them. It is in the background and is characterized by humility. Its discourse and behavior are surprising, to say the least, even incomprehensible for the common man. These are the holders of the initiatory or esoteric Tradition — the dynamic religion.

It is true that some particularly exceptional people are able to play the role of shepherds while also being holders of the esoteric Tradition. Only a certain level of accomplishment can allow the coexistence of these two types of "logic" inside the individual. One Cartesian, the other chaotic.

Is this true today for the leaders of the major religious and initiatory movements? It was certainly the case for Lao-Tzu, Shakyamuni and Jesus.

"I speak my mysteries to those who are worthy of my mysteries. What your right hand does, let not your left hand know what it does." —Gospel of Thomas 62

A "true initiation[1]" to the Tools is actually a privilege. In fact, unlike the "merchants of so-called spiritual products and methods"

----

1. A true initiation is about "how" to use the tool the "right way" and not "why," the answer to the latter is the lived experience and not the theory. Many levels of "how" exist depending on the level of the initiate.

that one can find in profusion today, an authentic Guide does not have the vocation to search for the applicant. He may even have a surly attitude, his role being to separate the wheat from the chaff. All Traditions respect this principle, as it is a question of respecting the dimension of the Spirit. It is therefore up to the Seeker to walk the path, and up to "fate" to make him meet the right person. Then, he will need patience, more patience, and even more patience, and gradually he will be able to access the different levels of initiation to the "tools."

A second parenthesis.

It is useful to point out something essential regarding the quality of the initiate. In fact, if he does not possess the required quality, the intended effect will only be partial, or even impossible. For example, in those traditions where one goes through the body, if the practitioner does not possess the necessary sensitivity, the Tool will only make him more effective, but he will plateau after that. The appearance will then be deceptive for the layman who will only see a very attractive façade.

So the layman looks at the finger, that is to say, the exoteric dimension. This is, by the way, one of the biggest temptations, the desire to stand out, to demonstrate, to appear. In the Yoga tradition, this is one of the last pitfalls to avoid — unfortunately, one can see that today...

However, if the required qualities are present, the Tool will accomplish its work and will allow the relation of body and Spirit so that one day the Other can present himself.

The moon will be seen, the esoteric aspect.

End of parentheses.

It is at this point that the initiate can consider himself a true disciple of a Tradition — *it is really important to clarify that an initiation is only the beginning of a new path, not an "accomplishment"; a rather common confusion, to say the least.*

Through his practice he will realize that Reason alone, the speculative, could not have helped him to find the desired path, the one

toward the opening of his field of consciousness. And because of
that, every time he was looking for answers among the various contemporary teachings offered, he was confronted only with intellectualization and emphatic speeches without any real interest. And
when he was shown the tools to use, the discursive approach was
limiting them and making them unproductive, because the theory
was the support for the work.

Lastly, the Tradition makes him benefit from the heritage received. It becomes a crucible where the transformation of his Being
can take place. He knows it, he verifies it, simply because his perceptive is being transformed. His relationship with what surrounds
him, with others, with the object[1], is modified in a subtle but sensitive way. Moreover, the exaltation that takes hold of him during his
work is real and palpable.

Each day brings him new sensations, a widened perception, a
new world. It is not Eden, nor bliss and happiness, smoke and mirrors so often promised to the layman, but rather an inner upheaval
that calls into question his initial understandings; an uncomfortable situation.

But this is manageable for him and does not disturb too much
his everyday life. He associates his "work with the tools" with the
definitions of ethics and the life principles of his Tradition. In addition, the "right" attitude begins to appear, but it still requires an
effort of will. However, this deliberate attention is captivating.

His quest is still egotistical without him being aware of it. The
underlying desire to be different, different from the others, which
the mask creates to avoid its own disappearance, develops to such a
point that very often it can sweep him away. A very effective trap,
because the tool begins to produce results. Charisma, the influence
of the right word, of the right gesture, pure intuition, all make the
Seeker's impact on the common man grow. From this feeling of
power an even more sufficient and more predatory Ego can arise,
synonym of an inevitable dead end.

1. Object: anything, animate or inanimate, that affects the senses.

It is at this point that the qualities of the Seeker must be present to counter this type of temptation. Very often, too often, we think the tool can and must do everything, including transform us, transform our mediocrity, our small limited "selves." This may be true, but is still wrong. It is true that the "right work" gives amplitude to the state of Being of the Seeker, but it is important to be careful, because depending on one's deep nature this can be: pretentiousness, aggression, hate, that is to say, Dark work — *and self-analysis remains difficult, to say the least, as always…*

It is also true that, by awakening his "sensitive Being," the Seeker can develop the root of love that is within him. And on the contrary, if in "everyday life" he continues to act in a shallow manner by being petty, envious and stingy, this root will quickly wither. To avoid this risk, it is necessary to self-observe without indulgence, not to be lenient toward oneself, everything must be done to progressively modify one's everyday behavior — *without forgetting to work daily with the bequeathed tools.*

Do it as if you were "someone else," an "other."

There is also a misunderstanding on this last point.

The error, quite common, to say the least, has as its origin the following precept: "To love others you must first love yourself." Most of the time, this is translated as "having a — blind — love for oneself, which allows one to love others." Unfortunately, if you apply this interpretation, it will only strengthen your egocentrism. In reality, the true meaning is the opposite; it is about correcting oneself so as to develop the qualities required for one's accomplishment, those related to one's state of Being and by extension, one's relation with others.

As a Buddhist sage used to say: "In order to wash your face, you must first clean the mirror," i.e., begin by being able to analyze yourself, to correct your thoughts and actions. Only then can the tools have an effect, the necessary qualities being present inside oneself.

You want the Other to awaken, to awake a part of the Divine inside you, to be Awakened, to unite with the Universe, the Tao,

God, to be One with the Whole, which are all fragmented expres-
sions of the Undefinable, and every day you act in a petty manner;
do not then ask the impossible from the Tradition, "After all, there
is nothing hidden that will not be revealed, and there is nothing
covered up that will remain undisclosed." —Gospel of Thomas 6
This is fundamental; the reproaches and reservations one can hear
about the quality of this or that tool, of this or that authentic Mas-
ter, are often the fruit of the mediocrity of the person uttering them.

Returning to the qualities; it is necessary to have an unshake-
able faith in one's quest, in the Tools, in the Tradition, and to give
oneself the means to advance on this path. To achieve this, an intimate principle must be applied. It consists in avoiding making
everything "about oneself." And therefore, as much as possible,
avoid talking about yourself, comparing yourself to others, acting
for personal well-being, for self-valorization — *for example, when*
one does a charitable act. And especially avoid wearing the mask of
the "Perfect one," the Philanthropist, who loves mankind. Instead,
one should rather tend toward humanism by having an altruistic
sensitive conduct, erasing any stereotype of predefined image and
becoming "transparent."

This behavioral evolution, which must progressively lead to a
state, cannot be understood without taking into account the following notions:

- Love cannot be a theory, because it emanates from deep within the Being. The love of the mother for her child is certainly
  the most obvious here. The fact of having been in unity with
  the fetus is certainly one of the roots of this feeling.
- Love for others cannot exist without awareness of the indivisible Unity; love is the force that leads us back toward it. And
  if one thinks, prematurely, to have achieved this state, the
  risk of believing oneself to be "accomplished" appears and
  with it the ensuing stagnation.

This feeling was skillfully expressed by the poet Baudelaire: "What is love if not the need to come out of one's self."[1]

The notion of Love is thus beyond individuality itself. Notion that we find in the religious texts as well.

- However, in some cases, the love for others itself can be the result of the conditioning received. As one writer said: "Do we love others for who they are or for the image we have of them?" The answer is not obvious if one is completely honest.
- As for the desire to do Good because of one's love for others, the above question can be readapted: "Do we love others for the image we have of ourselves?" And it is important to have the humility to express a reservation on any answer.

Same as Love, Good and Evil are difficult to define.

However, on this topic, it is possible to indulge in very abstract concepts, such as those that can be read in some contemporary Buddhist and Taoist works. For example, "Good and Evil are parts of an indissociable whole" or "Good and Evil do not exist because they end up meeting."

Of course, if we take the notion of the absolute where everything merges to form the Unity, any differentiation is wrong. However, is this within our dimension as living beings? The Vietnamese Buddhist monks who immolated themselves for the war to end, were they in the wrong? As for the child suffering the action of another person, should one feel nothing? During a visit to a concentration camp, is the dread one feels abstract?

If the answer is "Yes!," then the mask of Awakened that one is wearing has become an infirmity of the senses. A trap without a way out. But maybe sometimes rewarding; the unflappable attitude of the Sage? Or at least its caricature.

It is also possible to approach the notion of Good and Evil by saying in all logic, "Good is felt as Good, and Evil is felt as Evil." Perfect, but one must also define the criteria according to which the

1. Charles Baudelaire, *Mon Cœur mis à nu*, Éditions G. Grès et Cie, 1920, p. 114.

judgment is made. Is it based on religious, societal or philosophical morals and thus the result of the conditioning received? Or, is there actually a sensitive state allowing to perceive these notions?

Here again, if one is completely sincere, the answer is not obvious, as the conditioning received remains deeply anchored in each person.

Additionally, it must be pointed out that every Tradition transmits to the layman Seeker "a" moral which specifies the virtues to be acquired. A salutary precaution because working with the Tools allows to open oneself toward "particular fields of consciousness" that one can neither imagine, nor anticipate, so it might as well be guided beforehand.

Returning to the progression.

With the passing of time, a lot of time, thanks to the right work performed, a transformation of the "sensitive" happens. Through the opening of this sensitivity, of this breach, one day emerges "a certain permeability" of the field of consciousness to the Divine, the Unity, the undefinable. Previously, everything was only intellectualization of specific concepts, varying according to the origins it is true, but which remained definitions: "God is this, God is that, Awakening is this, Awakening is that, the Tao is this, the Tao is that, the path to follow is this one, the objective to reach is that one, the Perfect man is like this, the Awakened Being is like that.

Yet...

"To define God is to distance oneself from Him!" —*Prior of Mont des Cats abbey.*

"Whatever you may imagine God will be different!" —*a Sufi sage.*

"The Tao that can be told is not the eternal Tao" —*Lao Tzu.*

But now, this awareness is totally different because it is intuitive. It appears subtly and disappears without any way to control it. And every time, the recipient does not leave unscathed. He is distraught, sometimes tortured, by the inner struggle between his old convictions and his new perceptions.

> *This is reminiscent of:*
> *"He who seeks, let him not cease seeking until he finds; and when he finds he will be troubled, and when he is troubled he will be amazed, and he will reign over the All." —Gospel of Thomas 2*
> *The amazement is the beginning of the next step and perhaps the "reign" after that…*

But thanks to this antagonism, a new man emerges. A man who begins to realize that the paradoxes encountered cannot be answered without a sensitive approach, because Reason does not belong to the experiential.

Moreover, inside him appears a destabilizing, because unexpected, element: the "breath[1]." It runs through all or a part of his body, modifying the perception he had of himself. This "breath" — *called "presence of God" by some Christian monks* — is not only a physical perception, but is also linked to one's state of Being, to the Other.

Thus, the union of body and Spirit, which was previously only a theoretical principle, becomes awareness. However, the Seeker perceives this union as still partial. It is from this new state only — *"state of Being" and not yet "state of Soul/Spirit"* — that we can talk about Initiation. A real initiation because what happens inside the Seeker at this moment is a real evolution of the field of consciousness.

The layman finally becomes initiated, the embryo of his metamorphosis appears. From the speculative state where Reason was Queen, he finally reaches a sensitive state where the Spirit is King.

We must insist on this last point, as it is often forgotten.

The initiation cannot be only a carefully orchestrated play, in which the layman is a passive actor following a script created by men. This is so even if speculative analysis subsequently tries to demonstrate the contrary; it is a role play — *carefully orchestrated*.

The real initiation is the one that provokes the rupture of Rea-

---

1. "Breath," or Spiritus, Pneuma, Prana, Ruah, Ruh, Qi, Ki, is the "substance," the "presence" within oneself that allows the individual to join the undefinable in pure awareness — if "fate" is kind…

son so as to act directly on the sensitive dimension of the initiate, thus penetrating the unconscious — *for some, the deep brains.* Only this process can bring about a true metamorphosis of the layman — *just like the Koan can, when the Master questions the disciple at the propitious moment.*

> *Too often there is confusion between adherence to an institution holder of an authentic tradition through a Rite, and the "death of the layman" — initiation: teleutaion, to make die — considered as "an exit that gives access to a new dimension."*
>
> *The spiritual influence of the institution will only be achieved — in some cases — with quality, time and work, as it is most of the time...*
>
> *One may wonder if, for example, in some obedience of Freemasonry, this confusion does not come from an initial misinterpretation of the work to be done. This work consists in: "carving the raw stone so that it can be inserted in the common structure." Which is often interpreted as superficial work by an accumulation of "knowledge," so that the Freemason can integrate into society, that is to say, an exoteric work.*
>
> *However, on the spiritual level, it is better translated as: "learning to unlearn" as said by Lao Tzu, to find one's "inner Being" and join the All — universal structure, the One. In this last case, the "sensitive" produced by the Rite will be privileged and would precede any speculative work. The latter will only correspond to the acknowledgement of the sensitive states experienced. Esoteric work. But it requires daily work with a Tool of the Tradition.*
>
> *This confusion is common, and corresponds to a shortcut.*

Therefore a new "step" has been taken.

It is at this moment that the Seeker finds himself facing a new temptation, that to become a common man again. A desire which is a consequence of his inner feeling.

Indeed, the daily work done on himself has gradually melted the rigidity of his conformity. And because of that, his behavior, his points of view, appear as far-fetched to those around him. The simplistic theories, the syncretisms, the persona grata, which are presented in the media, in specialized books and at various conferences, produce in him an allergic reaction that he finds difficult to bear. As for the trendy "wisdoms" associated with them, they only aggrieve him. The classical topics of discussion, politics and sports, appear to him as the fruit of desperate agitation. Even social obligations, marriages and communions, if they are only emanations of the conditioning of the common man, become difficult to handle.

Moreover, observing the society that surrounds him only reinforces this feeling. The insignificance of human pretensions, of his own pretension, reveals itself to him and it is not an enviable situation. In consequence, the unconscious ill-being, which he was feeling deep inside, becomes a conscious ill-being, thus worsening the affliction.

Where is the time when there were no questions, no problems? Can this new State be buried under the old one? He almost wants it.

What he does not know yet is that, once this state has been reached, it becomes impossible to go back, because, as the Tradition states: "once the door has been opened, it cannot be closed."[1]

"I will destroy this house, and none shall be able to build it again."
—*Gospel of Thomas 71*

Fortunately, over time, it becomes possible for him to continue "playing his role" but this time while being aware of it; an uncomfortable position. So the Seeker takes refuge in his Tradition — *in the Tools received.* And it becomes his life. The other Seekers who share the path are, in his eyes, the only ones with whom he can exchange and comfort himself.

Something expressed in:
"Those here who do the will of my Father, these are my brothers and my mother…" —*Gospel of Thomas 99*

His path is Work and Ethic.

His quest is fierce determination.

---

1. An expression from the internal Chinese tradition.

THIRD STEP
MERGING INTO
THE ABSOLUTE

Time passes, the years go by, the daily work is done regularly. As with any sincere Seeker, the quest undertaken leads to varying states of mind. The Tools are working on one side, the life circumstances on the other, the moods fluctuate depending on the days and the moments. Periods of confidence are followed by moments of discouragement, and this emotional instability can sometimes bring about a certain resignation, a certain melancholy.

Contrary to what one may think — *or would it be better to say "to what one has read in the texts accompanying the so-called spiritual products on the market"* — this resignation is not negative. On the contrary, it allows the Seeker to lose the "rigid will," the "stone Spirit,"[1] which consists in "wanting to have," and above all it erases any egotistic and egocentric sentiment. This in turn produces the "right" state for working with the Tools.

> *This is not comparable to the acedia of Catholic theology, which is a spiritual ailment afflicting the monks of the desert and which manifests itself by boredom, lack of interest for prayer and discouragement; although...*

As a consequence, with time passing, one day, during work with the Tool, something undefinable happens within the Seeker. It is at this moment that his microcosm inside the macrocosm takes a new meaning.

---

1. TN: Stone spirit — by this image the author means a spirit locked in its certainties, its conditioning.

Up until then, all work done had as its basis individual accomplishment, at least according to his own interpretation. Which meant, according to the traditions encountered, to join God in Spirit, or to achieve Awakening, or to merge into the Tao, or into the Unity, or some beautiful theories, which he thought of as his own. However, formerly, deep inside him, these intellectualized concepts were only an echo, muffled and unknown.

But this time around, concretely, a part of "him" managed to escape, and the heavy cover of his individuation cracked somewhere. A bit like a dam too full that cracks, allowing only a small stream of water to escape — *which merges with "the sea of origin": which of the two merges into the other?*

But this stream has the taste of a tidal wave.

> *This is mentioned with a surprising transparency for "those who can read it" in:*
> *"I am the all; the all came forth from me, and the all attained to me." —Gospel of Thomas 77*
> *Or:*
> *"When you make the two one, and when you make the inside as the outside, and the outside as the inside,... then shall you enter the kingdom" —Gospel of Thomas 22*
> *"He makes the inner and the outer worlds to be indivisibly one." —Kabir*
> *Which is also found in Taoism, where the breath is approached in four steps, outlined as follows:*
> *"Refine the "vitality" into breath — the Jing into Qi, refine the breath into spirit — the Qi into Shen, refine the spirit into opening — external breath, internal Qi joins that external, "the spirit opens" — to then go toward the Tao."*

An experience beyond the abstractions that he has seen elaborated thousands of times:

- Analytically, making one think that the ineffable can be shown.
- In a tortured manner, using all kinds of clichés and stereotypes to explain the unexplainable.

The Seeker finds at this moment a beginning of the Cognizance that chases away the long accumulated knowledge. He realizes that everything is much simpler, more natural, than what had been described to him previously.

This "part" of him that has escaped is not a miracle as he had often been told. It is not a word, nor a text, nor a remark, nor a remarkable place, nor an exceptional encounter, nor a gesture or a prayer, that has acted. If it were only that, the readers of sacred texts, Christian, Buddhist, Hebrew, Hindu, Koans, the "Prayers" of all religions, the practitioners of any authentic Art would all have access to the same experience, without exception.

It is neither the Awakening such as it could have been described, that is to say, an opening of consciousness intended only for exceptional people — *knowing that losing one's individuality when it merges into the indivisible, by its nature, can only be a transitional state; then what to think of the constantly Awakened...*

No, it is rather one of the simplest experiences linked to one's own erasure! But he feels that a new "state of Being" has appeared in him, result of this overwhelming union.

This unknown perception will progressively make him question everything.

The first finding, the most important and the most distressing, is that it is not the "Self" that he had wanted. It happened, something else decided. He is, for once, connected to his essential Being.

In front of the evidence, he cannot but admit that his will, his Ego, cannot command in this realm. He finally understands that there is a hidden element in him, which is the link of Cognizance, linked to the Divine, the Universal, the One, the Tao, and that this link does not obey his orders.

> *Which is described in:*
> "*... He who knocks, to him will be opened.*"—*Gospel of Thomas 94*
> "*When you are at one with the Tao, the Tao welcomes you.*"
> —*Tao Te Ching 23*

On that day, this hidden element is revealed partially, breaking the barrier of his Reason, which was separating the "self" form the "outside of the self." It showed that it was the only Master; the "inner Master."

The most surprising for the Seeker is that this relative permeability has remained. As if this Union had transformed his perception and created a new sense. The consequence is an improved "sensitive" perception, which modifies his relation with what surrounds him, rendering "tangible" everything — nature, objects, the sounds heard and others.

But this would be a performance without much interest if it was not for another, even stranger, phenomenon. He remembers that during this "opening," he was able to perceive that his "internal breath," which has become "conscience / perception," has merged partially into the universal "indivisible breath." For him, his "Spirit" is now part of the indissociable whole. His "Soul breath" is thus linked for an "eternal moment" to his Spirit, a part of the universal.

> *"... To bring unity to all things in heaven and on earth under Christ."* —*Ephesians 1:10.*
>
> *Or, put differently:*
>
> *"The Tao produced One; One produced Two; Two produced Three; Three produced All things."* —*Lao-Tzu*
>
> *"One thing is all things; All things are one thing."* —*Master Sosan*
>
> *"For there are many first who shall be last, and they will become a single one."* —*Gospel of Thomas 4*
>
> *"Therefore I say that such a person, once integrated, will become full of light; but such a person, once divided will become full of darkness."* —*Gospel of Thomas 61*
>
> *"One with the One, one from the One, one in the One and, in the One, eternally One."* —*Meister Eckhart.*
>
> *"One is everything, everything is one."* —*Hermes Trismegistus*
>
> *"I am in everything, and everything is within me."* —*Kabir*

It is this "Soul-breath" that can link him, and then merge him with the Whole, with the Divine, with the Tao, with the inexpressible.

*From a certain stage the breath is guided by the Spirit, the breath
is Spirit.*
Kabir says: "O sadhu! God is the breath of all breaths."
Lao Tzu "... they are harmonized by the Breath of Vacancy."
—Tao Te Ching 42

But he knows that it is not an act of will. The "opening" only
happens when "he forgets himself," which is not letting go of mental control, but really self-effacement, erasing "one's own presence."

*Regarding the modern fashion of "letting go," of "mindfulness," of
"pure consciousness," of "Emptiness," etc. it must be known that,
rightly, Chan Buddhism ridicules such overdone images. Indeed,
"not thinking" can be a useful advice, but "non-thought" without
the work of a tool allowing to lead one's consciousness/perception,
allowing to generate a "transmutation" of the divided breath toward
that undivided — pneuma, "perceptive consciousness" — will only
produce "stubborn emptiness."[1]*

This can happen during a moment of "disillusionment" which,
in retrospect, is actually more of a partial realization of the truth.
Truth which makes him consider the insignificance of man, the
insignificance of his pretensions and the insignificance of his quest,
which will naturally find its answer in the final chaos; impermanence of all things and total illusion — *this is not about reasoning,
it is a state.*

"Be passersby." *—Gospel of Thomas 42*

At that moment, the desire to be superior to and different from
others, finally disappears. His "stone spirit," the one delimiting his
individuation, the one slowing him without him realizing it, progressively disintegrates, and through this breach the essential Being
can finally awaken.

The Seeker learns that it is this "stone spirit" that opposes his own
accomplishment. He is now aware that the "stone spirit" does not
leave him when he works inside some group, religious or initiatory,

1. Dalai Lama and Sheng Yen, *Meeting of minds,* Dharma Drum Publications, 1999.

or when he tries to act with utmost humility, or when he is inspired by sacred teachings, or when he works as best as he can with the tools of the Tradition. It is this "stone spirit" that reflects his desire to matter or possess. It becomes obvious to him that this "state of Being," a product of his egocentrism, was at the origin of his separation from the "Other." Previously, like most Seekers, he was telling himself that this was not the case, but this inflexible refusal was also evidence of the "stone spirit."

But from now on nothing will be simple, he guesses. The consciousness of this stubborn "presence" is so difficult to overcome to allow the opening of a breach, that dissolving it can only be the exception. Thus, he will have to focus his fight on the only enemy that can be defeated, which is yet another part of himself.

> *In all traditions, be they Western or Eastern, there is the universal symbol of the mirror. It is the greatest enemy one has to fight.*
> *Who is it?*
> *It is enough to look in the mirror!*

He will have to do it, not as in the beginning, "crudely," through a constant effort and the rigid will that accompanies it. But in a subtle manner, where the initial references are always deceptive, where his own mental presence can represent the most disabling burden.

Consequently, he knows that he must:

- Forget stubborn theories,
- Work gently and lightly, like a morning's breeze,
- Let the intuitive, the natural, express itself.

And above all:

- Seek no more to understand, but detach himself,
- Want no more to guide, but let himself be guided by "something else," by the Other.

Everything that is structure becomes a straitjacket. Straitjacket, the structure of any institution, expression of the "stone spirit." Straitjacket, the dress code, a representative aspect of any group; to him these are infantile disguises for role playing. Straitjacket, the clichés, the representations, the works, that pretend to be exceptional. Straitjacket, the images, the appearances, the tools modeled, that define the limits of an unfinished, because artificial, work. Straitjacket, the definition because a definition.

This detachment from any formalization is felt like a haven of peace, of love, of union. This is what finally lets him take a break, find a real rest, a well-being, a real well-Being. Finally, "He finds himself." Not in the sense of "finding one's little self," which would be of little interest, but rather in the sense of the persistence of perception that allowed him to "merge into the whole."

He can finally understand why this fusion is not negation, but infinite expansion, both physical and mental, which fades away to leave room only for the desired ecstasy. He senses it, he feels it intuitively, but the barrier that is his "stone spirit" still impedes him, even though it has been partially blurred.

For these reasons, for this reason, he frees himself from any rigid and alienating structure, even if this decision drives him away from loved ones. In this impetus, he eliminates any egocentric objective, like the numerous gratifying and attractive rattles offered to the common man, be they hell, heaven, future lives, Wisdom, Awakening or other promised dimensions.

> *Which is reminiscent of:*
> *"If those who lead you say to you: See, the kingdom is in heaven, then the birds of the heaven will go before you; if they say to you: It is in the sea, then the fish will go before you. But the kingdom is within you, and it is outside of you." —Gospel of Thomas 3*
> *"Heaven and hell are for the ignorant, not for those who know Hari." —Kabir*

He realizes that the list of seductive traps is much longer than he initially thought and that he should not overlook in it:

- Happiness, well-being, or the egocentric promises of all sorts,
- The pseudo-powers and abilities promised, such as healing or performing pseudo-miracles,
- The ranks, titles and rewards of all kinds.

Smoke and mirrors for the "well accomplished" who, thinking
that they have moved beyond illusions, get caught again into these
basic traps.

He realizes that all these lures are "empty illusions that will disappear with the death of the illusionist." But above all, they represent
the danger of falling back into the net, that is, of hardening one's
Spirit once again, and thus stagnating. Accordingly, he now knows
that he must:

- Practice without trying to achieve anything definite, without
  wanting to acquire proofs or rewards. To simply do it because
  he has Faith in the Union sought, the Fusion promised. The
  rest is superfluous, inconsistent, unimportant.
- Practice while forgetting the theory of the tools used, useful
  at the beginning, but which does not correspond anymore
  to the spontaneity of the attitude, of the word, of the gesture — *that is to say, the spontaneity of the Spirit.*
- Practice while abandoning the defined use of the mind
  which, with time, gave the "breath," so that the "breath" can
  become "free" of any attachment and thus join the exterior,
  the All, the Divine.

In short, the only thing that counts henceforth is the "right state
of Mind," or the "state of Soul."

But how difficult is the path!

As it is not "the self" that decides his future accomplishment,
there will be "days with and days without," he foresees it. So he has
to take into account:

- The people he interacts with — just like the allegory of the
  sheet which, when placed on manure or flowers, takes on
  their smell, animal mimicry acts just as much on men.
- His life principles — the initiate passes from a dogmatic
  moral to an ethic which, contrary to some definitions, must
  not be a "science of morals," but rather an "Art of guiding
  one's conduct." It must however be clarified that the latter
  is not a "know-how" but "the expression of a state of spiri-

tual accomplishment." The distant goal is to arrive at Virtue, product of the state of Soul, of a sensitive state. From this perceived state, a moral act will no longer be based on a religious moral or societal rightness, but because he will feel the necessity of it.

Thus, he realizes that his own notion of "Evil" will not depend anymore on:

- Religious laws and / or societal interdictions — *and threats*: level of the common man.
- His own self-interest — *hell-paradise, future life, rattle*: first step.
- The discipline of his thoughts that dictates it — *asceticism*: second step.

But in a sensitive and natural way, the "evil" felt by the other will be his own. Illusion? No, because this will only be a sensitive state rediscovered.

Confucius said, six centuries B.C.: "Do not do unto others what you do not want done unto you."

As always, some will tell him that his approach is wrong or of a very low level, because the canons of Enlightenment they have read indicate that "Awakening is the end of suffering!" or that "it is not the suffering that disappears, but the one that is suffering!"

Here again, he will find the ready made definitions that have become the "uniform" of thought for some. Of course, it is certainly true that the opposites meet, that Good and Evil are human perceptions, that there is no duality in the Universe since it is Unity.

In the absolute, certainly, but the human dimension is not the absolute, suffering remains a sensitive reality. To believe oneself living in a bubble of absolute during one's lifetime, thus identifying oneself with bookish references, can only be the result of a blindness due to egocentrism. Moving from compassion to empathy is related to the degree of the individual's sensitive evolution.

He was able to experiment that the more he was able to put aside his "little self," the more his empathy developed. And, the more the ego was present, the weaker his empathy was and his compassion nothing but an intellectual definition, consequence of his education.

> *It is also possible to accept the idea that an individual who has transcended his human nature would be able to "simply" don the state of the common man on occasion and to live a suffering which he himself has lost. A quality that appears implausible, that of Love — union / fusion — of which only Jesus, Buddha and a few select others would be capable.*

This is why it seems desirable to him not to put anything into drawers, such as "God is like this and not that," or "Awakening is this, the absence of it is that," or "the Tao is what I am describing."

From a certain point on, the paradox is the truth. And, as a consequence of this evolution, the dualism of opposition must give way to dualism, not Unity — *or suppression of dualism* — at least not yet, but to the "non-dual" whose association of opposites provokes the breakdown of binary analysis.

To do that, he looks again at the notion of Love — *the Love that is desire to come out of one's self, to make One with the other.*

The Love that is most often presented as positive can, same as the Good, have a negative action. The exclusive, oppressive love can become violence, murder, that is to say, "the Evil." However, the notion of Unicity, of initial Love, exists in both cases.

He realizes that the initial feeling is the same, however it can manifest itself in opposite ways.

In which box should Love be put?

Love is.

> *Only the notion of non-attachment allows to find a uniquely positive dimension to this feeling. However, non-attachment does not mean detaching oneself from others, but freeing oneself from the illusions attached to Love.*

But this is an outcome.

This initial non-judgment allows to apply the principle to any notion, for example:

- Fire: good — bad, light — burn, life — death.

The fire is.

- Death: fusion — separation, deliverance — pain, infinite — end.

Death is.

A principle that can be applied to anything...

This Seeker, who advances on the path, regularly seeks to regain the field of consciousness experienced, with the impression that it has left in him as a point of reference. This experience has allowed him to discover the truth inside him, which nobody but the Other, the Essential, the Divine, can provide.

Contrary to what he has often been led to believe, the path of a true spirituality does not lead man to distinguish himself. Quite the opposite, a single desire appears in him, that of blending in among his fellow men, not to stand out, not to be different, not to show his practice or his quest, so as not to return to his initial state — *monks from all religions apply this principle* — or almost.

The Seeker realizes that his accomplishment remains fragile until the fusion is achieved. He is not Awakened, nor Perfect, nor a Saint, all labels that he sees as storybook images for the layman. Accordingly, he avoids wearing:

- The physical uniform of "the man of Faith," of the "Awakened," of the Sage — *shown on magazine covers in beautiful poses and donning a circumstantial smile.*

How can one reach God, the One, the Tao, if the desire to distinguish oneself from what is common in everyday life is still present? "He is the greatest, because he is the humblest," was said of Jesus. "He turns away from the excesses common to all men," said Lao-Tzu.

- The stereotype "mental uniform" of "the man of Faith," of the "Awakened," of the Sage — *who remains undisturbed by the great events of life, who forgives everything to anyone, who develops stereotypes of wisdom.*

How to cultivate one's sensitive being with such a sanitized attitude?

Jesus chasing the merchants away from the Temple is a good example.

"So he made a whip of cords and drove them all out of the temple courts, with the sheep and the oxen. He scattered the coins of the money changers and overturned their tables." —John, 2:14-22

Obviously, this allegory means chasing away one's own greed from one's own temple and moving away from those carrying it, but with vitality and determination.

Even Gandhi, apostle of non-violence, stated that "fearlessness is the first requisite of spirituality" and that "cowards can never be moral."

From now on, he will be discreet and let himself be guided by his intuition, while taking care that the agonizing animal inside him does not regain its strength.

The third step of the path of the Seeker finally begins.

Where will it end?

What is the profile of the person who has accomplished it?

We will not pretend to answer these questions.

And above all, we will not make, as can too often be read, a syncretism of the clichés already written everywhere by those who did not always have the required experience.

It is enough to remind something that is a Secret inside many Traditions. This "last" step cannot be completed without becoming again an ordinary man. An ordinary man whose inner transformation occurs progressively and whose only desire is to merge into the whole. The accomplished Seeker thus drowns in the societal whole, eliminating any particularism — *just like the monk merges into his community to suppress any expression of his ego.* The alienating conditioning received is, at this point, nothing but a voluntary mask destined for society and the state of Soul that is awakening becomes his only spiritual guide.

This reminds the seven years of asceticism of the Buddha who, realizing that this is also a product of his ego, decides to move away from this type of mortification, which cannot but oppose his inner Peace, so he leaves his Masters. It is only after that, after recovering his lost energy thanks to abundant nourishment, and after retaking the aspect of an ordinary man, that he can find Illumination through meditation.

To draw a parallel with this allegory, it would be interesting to know the period of Jesus' life that has remained in the shadows, that of the Essenes known for their asceticism.

The question one might ask then is:

"Why has this level of work remained in the shadows?"

The obvious answer is that very quickly, even too quickly, the novice Seeker would don again the outfit of the ordinary man. But without the state being present, his "nature" will never allow his essential Being to express itself.

It should also be noted that, at this stage, it becomes possible to understand why the Tool is not sacred in itself, contrary to the assertions so often made. Any cult of the Tool is to be banished.

It is the Work that is sacred; the tool and the practitioner are to be forgotten. This is what the Seeker must keep in mind during this stage.

The tool produces the "Soul-breath," so that the "Soul-spirit" can emerge.

The importance given to the rest, to what is not part of the quest, is but a "rattle." The "rattle" allows the Tradition to draw the attention of the layman and, in parallel, the esoteric part remains in the shadows. But some laymen, having become Seekers, succeed in discerning a few shards of light in this darkness and find the "right" path.

This is why, the first humility to have is to tell oneself that one does not know, does not know anything. To avoid hindering one's unconscious, one's Mind must be open to all hypotheses. Obviously, this should not lead to credulity, it is about keeping a mind open to any possibility, knowing that experience will one day confirm or refute it. Just like the subjective part of your mind makes believe in individuation, corporeal and spiritual, it can also obscure the awareness of the Seeker of his surroundings.

In addition, it should be emphasized that the experience of an opening of one's "field of consciousness" allows to erase many certainties:

- About the effect of the "thought Soul / Spirit" on our environment, on others, on oneself,
- And hence, the action of the prayer,
- But also, and unfortunately, about the effect of thought on "the Dark work,"
- About the importance of the life of other species relative to ours, about their relationship, their dependance, our dependance, the universal interdependence. But here again, it is necessary to reject any "role play," only empathy, daughter of the state of Soul must guide one's conduct. Empathy which allows to understand that "non-attachment" should concern only the rejection of illusory material values.

The Seeker finds himself then at the center of a difficult perception, that of universal suffering, that of Man being capable of the best but also and above all the worst toward his fellow men, as well as toward everything that surrounds him, animal, insects, nature. Without forgetting the environmental macrocosm, where each species feeds on the weaker, at every moment, without a break of any kind.

Of course, in contrast a sunrise is wonderful, a child's laughter enchanting, as are the eyes of one's dog.

We find here the symbol of the cross, where the "awakened" is torn between the vertical — a notion of absolute — and the horizon-

*tal — his human condition, entirely relative. Are we to under-
stand here the last words of Jesus: "My God, my God, why have you
forsaken me?"*

This uncompromising discernment makes it possible to understand why the great religious movements have built a conditioning for the common man, because as everyone can see, the latter
does not have the faculty of empathy or compassion required to do
without the dogma and without the laws. The examples are legion,
and despite the legal constraints and moral laws, it seems impossible to make an exhaustive list.

Even where religion establishes itself, the superstition of the common man reemerges. Instead of seeking the esoteric aspect contained within, man will venerate the authorities, knock on wood,
drink water, kiss the idol, all in an uncontrolled mess.

Nevertheless, observing this tragicomedy does not have a negative impact on the experienced Seeker. On the contrary, it creates
in him the necessity to bathe himself regularly and in awareness in
the universal harmony that he feels intimately every time he works
on himself. This harmony, where everything is suspended inside
the unicity, outside of time and of any individuality. He then wishes that the complete immersion would occur one day, so that he
could join for an eternal moment the ineffable. Extracting himself
from his relative condition becomes vital, a paradox par excellence.

*A sensitive state that can only strengthen the inner impetus along this
last stage.*

THE OPERATIVE WORK

To begin with, what do we classify under the term "Operative tools"? These are, at the same time, the methods, processes, exercises and disciplines whose objective is to allow a person to reach some level of knowledge, in our case spiritual.

"Knowledge" in this case means the product of a "sensitive experience" allowing to widen one's field of consciousness and perception in a "dimension" that the five senses, Reason, the present state of mind, the unconscious and science cannot apprehend. This "dimension," which cannot be defined, is often expressed through symbols like the following: God, Lord, Father, Divine, Alpha and Omega, Great Architect, Tao, Unity, All, Ineffable, indescribable…

These Tools come from the Primordial Tradition, which itself comes from the dawn of time, an era when Man still had an intimate relationship with the indefinable. The different religious and initiatory traditions carry vestiges from the West, the East and the Far East, which appear to be different but their basic work is identical. An essential point to remember is that these Tools are double sided. The exoteric side, known by everyone, made for the layman, and the esoteric side, "hidden," intended for those who seek. The difference lies in the "Know-how," that is to say, the application of the principles, the rules allowing for a progressive learning of the methods, procedures and exercises.

The process of evolution of an authentic quest requires the "right" use of these Tools, as previously said. To that end, to achieve the necessary competence, the Seeker must find a Master of the Tradition, or an experienced Seeker who will be able to initiate him in the progressive learning of the "Know-how." After that, *a detail* not to be overlooked, this Master must perceive in the seeker the qualities required to receive his teaching — *which we will address later.*

Finally, if the qualities are present, the initiator will take into account the level of achievement of the seeker, his existing "field of consciousness," so as to be able to communicate a compatible level of teaching. In addition, it must be noted, a subtle union is progressively created between the man and the Tool during the work done; it can be called synergy. For this to occur, an adjustment of both the mind of the user and the procedure applied is indispensable. These are the main reasons that justify the secrets surrounding the different levels of initiation.

In fact, man unconsciously apprehends the ephemeral nature of his condition, and because of that he is restless in trying to obtain what he desires. Furthermore, it should not be forgotten, any individual, even those Seeking, possesses a natural inclination toward egocentrism, which leads him to overestimate himself.

For these reasons, the Master — *who should rather be called "The one who is in front" on the path, the Guide* — is supposed to provide each step of the progression in a "piecemeal" fashion. For, as a notion to be underlined, an initiation to the Tool that is not in adequacy with its user will be totally inoperative.

> *The question that every layman asks at some point is:*
> *"How to recognize an authentic Master?"*
> *The answer is: "it is impossible."*
> *Impossible, because the quality of an authentic Master is so subtle that the seeker who does not yet have a "sufficient" level of accomplishment, cannot perceive it. However, it is possible to eliminate the more obvious impostors — whether aware of being such or not — by applying the following filters:*
>
> - *First criteria: the Master is not greedy. Your relation with him is not linked to financial elements or various interests; power, influence, sex, image, etc.*
> - *Second criteria: he is not interested in showing off. He does not let photos be taken of him in ego-gratifying poses, does not boast about his qualities in the media, does not look for honors and awards.*

- *Third criteria: he does not constantly shake the rattles of his school, does not promise bliss, immediate Happiness, a dream-like afterlife, various abilities, etc.*

The authentic Masters would thus be very few...

You have noticed that we did not mention the criteria often used by anti-sectarian associations: "He must not influence your family life." Ask yourself this question: "How can a spiritual quest not influence your private life?"

In the following lines we will look at the most common Tools and their operating procedures linked to the previously described symbolic stages.

THE PRAYER

The prayer is certainly the most instinctive act when man wishes to connect with God, a Divinity, the Tao, the All — *which we will call the Divine in this chapter.* And consequently, it is the most shared Tool of the religious and initiatory traditions.

The prayer of the common man, when within the frame of a structure, is formal both on the level of expression and form. Most of the time it is done more by respect for a learned and reproduced rite than to answer an inner "thirst"...

By inner thirst we mean a necessity felt deep within oneself and not the desire to acquire things like: well-being, material goods, future life, powers of all sorts — which are, as a reminder, rattles destined for the layman.

The Divine one prays to is an omnipresent abstraction; at this stage it is recitation.

The Divine one prays to, God, Father, Buddha, a divinity, a saint, an entity, is the personification of this abstraction which is thus omnipotent and ineffable — *a paradox par excellence.*

The prayer of the layman can be defined as an action wanted by Reason, in the hope that this action produces an effect, either on one's fate or on one's Spirit. The rite has its reasons that Reason understands and this is what motivates the "paying person."

Thus, the prayer is seen by the layman as a magical and ritual performative formula — *performing an action by the fact of its formulation*. It is formal and varies according to the different religious schools. It is an incantatory formula.

The prayer of the Seeker who is beginning his quest is Rite and discipline of an initiatory religious school. He prays because the "right" act of prayer allows him to bypass his mental and touch his "Profound,"[1] or the "Other" inside oneself.

Form is sacralized, gestures and words are discipline.

The prayer participates in the creation of the "breath Soul / Spirit."

It is the beginning of communion.

The Divine one prays to is inside oneself and outside oneself; it is immanence that must lead to transcendence. It is foreseen. The prayer is animation of the "Profound."

The prayer of the accomplished Seeker is "Soul-Spirit." It is "state of Soul," a communion close to fusion. It is the form and the non-form, the form becoming humility and self-abstraction.

As a reminder, Jesus was praying "without form":
- *On his knees (Luke 22:41)*
- *His face to the ground (Matthew 26:39)*
- *Looking up (Mark 7:34, John 11:41)*
- *Rejoiced (Luke 10:21)*

The Divine one prays to is "communion" — *connecting with and then one day merging into the All.* It is felt — *foreseen* — but not yet experienced. The prayer is an emanation of the "essential Being."

A rather poor synthesis compared to reality, but it allows to get an idea of the possible evolution of a praying person.

---

1. By "Profound" the author means the transcendent spiritual dimension hidden inside every person.

The prayer of a desperate man allows to establish a "relation" of a quality far superior to any ritualistic approach, even one of a high level, because the "state of Soul" is spontaneously attained.

"Blessed is the man who has suffered; he has found life." —Gospel of Thomas 58

The greatest quality of the prayer is the acceptance of the state of self-effacement. In all traditions, the praying person submits to the will of "something else": the Divine, a cosmic order, inexpressible and indefinable. And from this state, man has the possibility to comprehend his condition, his impermanence, his illusion.

The entire formal attitude of the prayer is based on this notion.

Whether he stands, kneels or prostrates himself, man dissolves into the sought-after union, with the "stone spirit" disintegrating.

The full intention of the Being is focused in one direction in the hope of coming out of oneself and merging with the Divine, the Tao. The mask, the ego, the Persona, all fall and the resurrection of the "Other," of the Divine inside oneself, can occur.

The "inner breath, Soul / Spirit," lead by the exaltation of this communion, can merge in awareness with the undivided one. The barrier of individuation disappears for an "eternal moment" and the transmutation can happen.

Exceptional, of course!

Lastly, let us make it clear to those who would bow only to God that in prayer they submit themselves from the smallest to the greatest, from the humblest to the most brilliant, from the micro to the macro, and that their vanity is nothing but illusion.

THE MEDITATION

Let us begin by correcting one of the most common errors, once again a consequence of the limits of the definition.

To meditate does not mean only to submit oneself to a long reflection — *latin root "meditari"* — that is to say, to examine more thoroughly an idea, as explained in our dictionaries. This would still concern Reason and would be totally opposed to the principle of the Tool.

Some of today's schools quote another latin root, using Sanskrit as a support — *"mederi" and "madya"* — and come to the conclusion that the objective of meditation is to "take care of the center of one's being." The goal of this interpretation is to be understandable to everyone and above all attractive on the marketing level; which is also the primary objective of all "contemporary products" related to meditation — *those promising "well-being," or even "Happiness," wisdom etc.*

However, to remain respectful of the Tradition, we will translate it as "being lead toward the center" — *same as translated by Karlfried Graf Dürckheim*[1].

> *It should be mentioned that the center is not "the self," but the link inside oneself that leads to the Divine, the One, the Tao.*
>
> *"Know thyself, and thou shalt know the universe and God." Temple of Apollo at Delphi*

There is also a second error to be corrected, an obvious one. The body position — *in other words, "the Spirit being guided and controlled by the postural sensitivity of the meditation"* — is not unique. The most common one is that seated, in lotus or half-lotus — *the stereotype image of meditation for the layman.*

> *On this subject, in the East it is clarified that to meditate the eyes should not be completely closed. A western "specialist" taught it necessary to indicate that this was due to the fact that Easterners*

---

1. Karlfried Graf Dürckheim, *Hara, the vital center of man,* Inner traditions, 2004.

fall asleep more easily. A rather limited assessment, to put it mildly. The actual reason for not closing one's eyes is completely different, in fact, the "presence" must progressively be both inside and outside the body, with the two merging on the sensitive level.

Meditation can also be done while standing without visibly moving. Details vary between schools.

Or, while moving, for example, slow walking. Even seated on a chair or lying down for those with a physical weakness.

In fact, a paraplegic person, or someone with a deformation of the spine, or any other physical issue, can also meditate; obvious but useful to point out…

This is why the widely known and quoted Zen saying "posture is fundamental" does not mean, as is often interpreted:

- That the sensitive perception of a specific posture is the main notion to be sought — *awakening of the awareness / perception of one's interiority* — *the apprentice level, first stage.*

But rather that the work must lead to a perception of the "breath Soul / Spirit" inside oneself:

- It allows to "silence the reflective" and to "forget oneself" in the posture — *second stage.*
- To finally arrive at "the melting of the self and forgetting the posture" so as to be lead — *merge* — into the "undivided breath," or the Tao — *third stage.*

As always, it is not desirable to stop at the finger which, in this tool, is of course the "form" — *without forgetting the self-image.* So, what should one make of those *"masters"* who demonstrate with solemn expression the quality of their posture? We leave the answer to you.

In Chan — or Zen, or Tantrism — it is said to "sit without purpose." Trying to detail and analyze the state of Awakening, that is, to define Awakening, indicates the desire to obtain. The Awakening becomes an objective and because of that the Spirit becomes "Stone," an insurmountable obstacle during mediation.

The desire to obtain must disappear — to want without want-
ing — but the inner fire must exist — the paradox of a state that
one does not choose.

The meditator must be "guided" by the "Impetus of the profound."
Lao-Tzu's allegory about the "right" state of mind for meditation is
exemplary in its precision:

"I alone don't care,
I alone am expressionless,
like an infant before it can smile." —Tao Te Ching 20
Jesus, regarding the state to tend to:
"These nursing babies are like those who enter the (Father's) king-
dom." —Gospel of Thomas 22

Based on the above, what to think of the contemporary sophisti-
cated developments that mix intellectualism, philosophy, psychism
and (pseudo) spirituality?

Each school practices meditation differently, but it is possible to
recognize in all of these traditions a common essence, specifically
the notion of "letting go." However, to avoid the usual banalities,
this principle, or rather state to be achieved, requires a progressive
approach.

Let us begin with the common man:

He meditates for leisure or for the purpose of "well-being": to
unwind, to de-stress, to escape his context, to recharge or for a
"predefined spirituality" — *understandable goals*. In certain arts of
the gesture — *martial arts, yoga,…* — the goal is to improve one's
performance: to have the most beautiful and demonstrative posture, to be the most "beautiful" or the strongest — *obviously egocentric dead ends.*

The meditation methods are diverse: breath work, reflection on
a certain topic, imagination, images, attention toward an object,
non-developed intention of the gesture, mental relaxation, etc.

A common mistake regarding the above: physiological breathing
can be a Tool — for example, Pranayama. But it should not be
confused with the "breath," a substance that is the matter used

and which evolves over time in 4 stages: solid, liquid, gaseous and finally ethereal, becoming "awareness/perception, Soul/Spirit," divided breath toward undivided breath — Prana/Atman/Brahman. However, physiological breathing can be used as a "Tool" that can guide the "breath," same as the gesture, the sound, etc.

For the Seeker, the first stage passes through Reason.

At first, he gathers the existing theories on the subject, through reading, specialized conferences and seminars. After that, he tries to apply them during his meditation — *knowing that they vary between schools.* However, at some point, he realizes that they all share the same purpose, to overthrow the mind in order to touch the essential Being, the "Profound," the Other that is within. He also notices that very often, too often, he is told that the final objective is the famous "Awakening" — *which becomes "the dream of the sleeping."*

The next stage begins when the Seeker stops believing this premature dream and realizes that if this transmutation is to happen one day, it can only be the consequence of a very, very long work. He then invests himself in it, his quest becoming essential.

Hours of mediation add up and a truth appears, concerning the "right" work — it is simplicity and moderation.

So he intuitively turns toward a tradition of the barest, which does not promise anything except a work without artifice. He thus frees himself from anything superfluous that hinders him.

Then, progressively, the "breath/Spirit" emerges and becomes work itself. The "breath" becomes a palpable substance and time stands still. The will guides the ascesis, but the "inner impetus" awakens.

One day, one moment, the beginning of the third stage takes place.

The work done has allowed the connection between the "breath" and the "state of Being." Only this state appears "right" to the meditator. The will fades and gives way to the state. Enlightenment is seen as an egotistic will, or an egocentric direction. To be awakened or not, such a classification can only make him smile.

Now only the call of the "Profound" is expressed as an unquenchable thirst that guides the meditator. The Self, the others, the Other, the essential Being, all disappear leaving only a universal presence. "The Presence" is meditation.

Regarding the fusion…

The sensitive permeability of body and Mind achieved allows for an exchange between interior and exterior, a communion, but not yet fusion. The Seeker perceives sensitively that the fracture between the Being and the Universe, between the Being and the Divine, is only subjective and can completely disappear. But he feels that there remains in him a tiny tension, a "zest" of this "stone spirit," which prevents him from merging and receiving. He is on the razor's edge of his own presence, which seems fragile and the rupture feels imminent.

He has to let go more and more, and maybe tomorrow, or after tomorrow, the fusion will happen.

This does not depend on his will…

THE KOAN

We hesitated on whether to mention the Koan in this chapter and this despite its popularity nowadays.

For the neophytes, let us point out that the Koan is, or rather should be:

- An exchange between a Master and his disciple — *most often a question from the Master for his disciple* — impossible to understand by reason only. The theoretical aim is to awaken the Other, the essential Being, through what some call an "apostrophe of the profound."

The most classic example is:

"What is the sound of a tree falling in an empty forest?"

This type of question is supposed to produce a break in reason so as to touch directly the essential Being and provoke the Awakening. This may be possible — *in a "heart to heart" exchange, at the ad hoc moment, and depending on the subject...*

However, when a person becomes used to this type of questions — *especially with the publication of books explaining and dissecting the Koan* — his Reason, far from being fooled, knows how to react opposite to the education received. A bit like a mirror reflecting an object. From that moment on, the Koan loses its impact on the intuitive and only the "Reason mirror" responds; which is an intellectual game.

> *It is for this reason that the Chinese monk Zhaozhou answered "No!" to the koan "Does a dog have Buddha-nature or not?" while the Mahayana doctrine, of which he had a perfect grasp, states that "all beings have Buddha-nature." With his answer, which was outside any logic, the Master meant that there could be no doctrine, no definition, no explanation in the approach to Awakening.*
>
> *The books trying to "explain" the Koan go against the principle itself, but everyone has his own opinion...*

Lastly, there is an important element that everyone seems to forget. It is the human dimension. The Koan is made by a Master for his disciple. It is directly connected to both the "heart to heart" relation between them and the specific sensitivity of the disciple. The Master expresses the Koan at the moment when he perceives an opening in the mental conditioning of his disciple. Using the propitious moment allows to disorganize the mind, Reason and logic, so as to penetrate the "Profound" and cause a break useful to the Awakening of awareness. Extracting the Koan from this context cancels its function; its effectiveness cannot exist without the communion of the two Beings.

Some texts of the Christian tradition resemble the Koan of the Far East; for example, this one from the Gospel of Thomas: "Be passersby!"

The Koan must act like a shock, like a slap, only then is the break of Reason possible.

But without the "groundwork" of meditation beforehand, it can only be unproductive.

THE MANTRA

The mantra is a repetitive sacred formula addressed to a divinity or Buddha — *knowing that the historical Buddha said that he was "a man like any other" — or almost...*

The transmission of a Mantra is often wrongly presented as an initiation. An initiation, it has to be reminded, must be a lived experience bringing to the initiate the "emotion" of a real change of state of consciousness.

The mantra can be compared to a prayer. To clarify, the common man believes in the "magical" power of the mantra and venerates it as such. To remain positive, it could be considered that some traditions use this subterfuge to arouse the interest of the layman. Accordingly, the recipient will consider the object — *the Mantra* — as sacred, and therefore will work with the tool for an "immediate" result — *just like the Abracadabra of the Greek tradition.*

Here is a quote from a Buddhist "expert" as an example:

"A mantra is not a kind of prayer addressed to a divine being. Rather, the mantra is the deity, the enlightenment immediately manifested."

Not only do we find the notion of dualism in this definition, the opposition prayer mantra, but also the idolatrous belief in the object. Yet the object, the mantra in this case, only has value if it fuses with the practitioner, and the practitioner fuses with the "All," the Divine, so that the Work can occur.

Kabir, "the awakened poet" makes a mockery of this type of attitude:

> *"The parrot repeats the name of God,*
> *Without knowing anything of his greatness!"*

Supported by this aim, over time, the layman will have to progressively transcend the object, the Tool, to become a Seeker and approach the indefinable, the inexpressible — *at least one can hope so.*

In the preceding lines, we find again the common confusion between the means and the "objective."

The first stage is the understanding, through Reason, that the repetition of the mantra keeps the mind "busy," thus allowing the Other to come out, more or less.

The second stage begins when the "breath" appears, generated by the sound and the directed intention. The opening of the consciousness is foreseen.

The third stage is when the "sound / breath / Spirit" of the Mantra becomes the support for the communion with the "undivided breath" — *the beginning of the path toward a possible fusion.*

In conclusion: the Mantra is a tool that uses the sound.

THE SOUND

As we already mentioned, the Mantra is one of the tools that use the sound to guide the "breath, Soul / Spirit," same as the throat singing from central Asia — *overtone singing* —, the Islamic Dhikr — *a rhythmic repetition of the name of Allah* —, the Hindu Japa — *a "yoga" technique based on a very long repetition of the name of a divinity* —, the Chinese Shi Sheng or the Japanese Kiai — *work with the sound with a "martial aim"* —, the Japanese No — *at its origin* —, and the liturgical chants.

It should be noted that today most of these traditional techniques have been diverted from their initial objective of spiritual Awakening. In fact, the current tendency is to make them pleasant for the audience with the idea to market them and extract a profit — the merchants of the temple, as always.

*This desire for profit makes the operating mode disappear and it
will disappear perhaps forever, the essential principles of work being lost — as is the case for many traditional tools...*

This type of work is not about playing with phonemes, as it is
often presented, but about finding the principles of the previously
mentioned tools. The aim is to pull the "breath / Spirit / substance"
from the interior to the exterior, so that one day the communion
can occur.

"He makes the inner and the outer worlds to be indivisibly one."
Kabir

IN CONCLUSION OF THIS CHAPTER

Through these examples we tried to illustrate something that can
only be experienced. Any explanation or description of a lived experience can only be a pale reflection of reality. And only the practice with traditional tools under the "heart to heart" teaching of a
Guide can give access to the experience.

Nevertheless, as we tried to explain it, the main thing to remember is that the essence contained in the "know-how" of each tool of
any authentic tradition is identical. Its role can be summed up this
way: to transform the progressively perceived "breath / Soul" — *the
presence of God in some Traditions* — into "Breath / Spirit" so that
one day, one moment, it can merge into the "undivided breath" of
the Divine, the Tao, …

The Carthusian monks do seven hours of daily prayers.
*Is it meditation or prayer, or both? Or, is it "only" an expression of
the same "desire to be led"?*

Often, men let themselves be caught in the trap of belonging to a
group or an institution, expression of their instinct of a gregarious
animal, and thus find themselves at a dead end. This uncontrolled
instinct leads them to think that only their community holds the
Truth; the truth about the tool, the truth about the method, the
truth about the Spirit, the truth about the Soul, the truth about the

Divine, the truth about the ineffable.

The examples are endless. In Zen Buddhism, the Soto and Rinzai sects are opposed on the definition of meditation but, as any sincere Seeker discovers, the "right" meditation loses any definition over time.

The Form is just the shell that covers the essential, why argue about it? Maybe for the sake of more adherents and power?

This example can be reproduced infinitely, it is enough to observe the opposition existing between the great religious movements or between the smallest obediences. Without forgetting the infighting inside every institution where every person holds the truth of the Truth.

This is certainly the reason why some experienced Seekers choose not to belong to any institution or structured group, thus remaining spiritually unhindered.

THE ARTS

To begin with, let us specify what "Art" should not be. In the way we understand "Art," it cannot have a lucrative purpose. The latter imposes an obligation to conform to the tastes and trends in the society and thus forces the artist to create a conventional expression. Consequently, Art should not be an "expression of beauty," as it can be defined today by society.

Thus, the work of an artist can displease those who do not have the "quality" to perceive the sensitive dimension expressed, and so it can remain unrecognized as a "work of art" by the critics. Art is not always an expression of "know-how" or a high level of technique. Art is not a product of the intellect.

And let us specify what Art should be. Art is an expression of the sensitivity of the artist, of his interiority. The artist obeys an inner impetus that drives him and guides him — *his inspiration or Muse*. Art can be skill, competence or mastery in a particular field, qualities linked to one's accomplishment. However, paradoxically, a work created without virtuosity is still Art, even if it does not seduce the layman.

After a certain level of accomplishment, Art is the emanation of the essential Being, or in other words, an expression of certain spiritual transcendence.

Art is a tool of accomplishment.

Art is the product of accomplishment.

Let us look at a few examples.

POETRY

A dictionary will tell you that poetry is an Art of the language aiming to express rhythm, harmony and image.

As always, one can see that the definition limits the object, which corresponds to the very reference of the received education. It is therefore not surprising to note that, during our school education, it was imposed on us to interpret and analyze the verses of certain poems. The technique taught consisted in dissecting each word and each line, while taking account of the social and economic context of the time, as well as the life and personality of the poet. Based on this binary analysis, it was possible to create an explanatory summary.

One can see that, if there was a desire to suppress the sensitive rush of the poet, it would be difficult to do better.

This is still true today, and the educational system still does not care, forgetting:

- What Cocteau was saying: *"Poetry stops at the idea, any idea kills it."*
- And Éluard: *"What has been understood no longer exists."*

Consequently, the common man will have an analytical approach to the text and, logically, will not be very sensitive to the expression of the poet, unless the latter writes specifically to please, by expressing images that conform to the expectations of the "art critics." In this last case, what will emerge from the work will be "the stereotype of the sensitive," which will then be commented on and appreciated. But is it still poetry?

In contrast, when using a sensitive approach it becomes possible to perceive that the path taken by some poets, thanks to their art, can be likened to an initiatory quest. The evolving expression of the poet thus becomes the tool that shapes the "breath / Spirit", the work leading to the Work.

One of the most beautiful images about poetry is certainly that of the Chinese poet Ong Giao Ki: *"Poetry is the sound of the heart."*[1]

Jalāl ad-Dīn Muḥammad Rūmī did just as well on the poet:

"The poet is the man of the Threshold of the Worlds, the mute speaker. That is it! The secret is revealed, Enough, silence!"[2]

The stages of accomplishment of the "poet in quest" can be described as follows:

First of all, as already described, there is an inner fire inside him that he must express one way or another, and his inspiration makes him want to write. Because of his structuring education, the amateur poet will try to construct his work with his Reason. He will decide on a subject, develop it rationally and dissect the effect sought with his words and the structure of his verses, as he was taught by his eduction. He will study the rhyme and will define a rhythm by using a dictionary of rhymes — *for poets in need of inspiration.* After some time, he will notice that in the poems constructed in this manner, no rush, no Heart, no impulse of the Profound was expressed and this, despite all the work done.

Then, one day, guided by his state of Soul, suppressing the role of his Reason, his hand begins to write words out of nowhere. And, becoming aware of the text, he realizes that an Other has expressed himself through him, through the self.

This is why the apprentice in quest speaks of a "poet's soul" or of his Muse as something innate, immanent or transcendent, without really knowing what it is. But his Muse allows him to express the inexpressible thanks to the sensitive images put down on paper. Work which revives the "Profound" in him. "Accomplished" Poets have an extreme sensitivity that goes beyond what is common, a vision or a perception that seems supra-sensorial. It is this vision that appears on the paper and that allows them to be "right."

1. Henri Borel and Dwight Goddard, *Lao-Tzu's Tao and Wu Wei*, Cosimo Classics, p. 81.

2. Rumi, *Le livre du dedans*, Edition Albin Michel, 1997.

Obviously, the described dimension is in total opposition to the willful approach of the poets "à la mode," those who write for a living, and not to survive, who write to please the media and the clients. They make believe in the sensitive, by developing a demonstrative sensibility through stereotyped images whose aim is to move or enchant a particular age group or social category. A sensitivity of the ego put in rhymes, and very often in music nowadays.

But this was also true yesterday; it is enough to mention the Romanticism. Ronsard, who was liked by Henri II and then Charles IX because of his works of "good taste," was declared "Prince of Poets" — *more smoke and mirrors.* But he was able to transcend his art when he wrote, toward the end of his life, about his physical suffering and his Christian faith in the face of death.

In fact, what characterizes most poets of quality are certainly the torments of their lives — *which was also often the case for certain Saints and Awakened.*

"Blessed is the man who has suffered; he has found life." —Gospel of Thomas 58

The suffering felt or perceived in the other — *often a "loved one"* — allows to "open" one's sensitivity and reach the Other inside oneself. Sakyamuni, the historical Buddha, is the perfect example. As everyone knows, the contrast between his life as a Prince, made of ease and well-being, and the discovery, when he left the palace, of the misfortunes of life, was the trigger for the beginning of his quest.

This beautiful story is most probably a parable about this "opening" of the sensitive. The palace represents one's egocentrism that one must leave to become aware, through empathy, of the suffering of the people encountered. A first step toward the opening of one's field of consciousness. In other words, to move from egocentrism to allocentrism.

However, for most people, only their own suffering will allow this metamorphosis. It remains a possibility, because conversely this type of hardship can lead to an undesirable path of self-destruction. Rimbaud, Verlaine, Villon, all exceptional poets, have demonstrated it. They lived bohemian lives of violence and all sorts of excesses, joined by Baudelaire toward the end of his life.

It is certainly the inner trauma and "ill-Being" felt, consequence of the fight between the mask that was imposed upon them and its rejection through the excess — *product of the inner torment* — which was at the origin of their talent, but also of their misfortune.

> *To quote Doctor MacLean:*
> *"In looking at the neural mechanisms that underlie the sense of our own reality, I pay particular attention to the type of aura experienced by Dostoevsky and described in the "Idiot" as: "a feeling of existence to the most intense degree."*[1]
> *This feeling of exacerbated existence is probably that of the "cursed poets."*

Presumably, their "Muse," part of the "Other," was able to express itself, but unfortunately the abuse of psychoactive substances hindered their "spiritual Impetus."

This type of disharmony can also be found in other Arts.

The dance with Nijinsky who succeeded in transmitting the non-transmittable, the horror of the war, but who was afflicted by madness.

The Chinese internal arts where excesses of all sorts — *alcohol, drugs* — punctuate the lives of the most illustrious Masters. The danger is great when there is an inner dissonance.

Some exceptional poets have succeeded in transmitting "a sensitive message." A "palpable" dimension, which communicates an expression that can be "lived." For example, the Japanese Haiku. Poems composed of 17 syllables, divided into 3 verses — 5-7-5 — which illustrate not the totality of the Zen spirit, as it is often said — *the Zen spirit should be silence* — but the pared-down transmission of a perceptive emotion.

1. Paul D. Mac Lean, Roland Guyot, *Les trois cerveaux de l'homme*, Éditions Robert Laffont, 1990.

The principles applied are as follows: no complexity, no discrimination, no intellectualization and no agitation. But possibly only the Form is opposed to this non-intellectualization — *constraint of the form, which should become "natural" for the seasoned poet...*

The Haiku has the quality to communicate "heart to heart" the sensitive state of the poet. The image is immediate, just like the feeling generated; it is. It cannot be explained, it is not possible to dissect the "why" — *without forgetting that translating is...*

To quote one of the most famous Haiku, the one from Basho:

"The old pond
A frog leaps in.
Sound of the water."[1]

We will avoid, as is too often the case, opposing traditions, by quoting Rimbaud whose "drunken boat" resembles in this example the spirit of the Haiku — *even though this may surprise some cynics*:

"A squatting child full of sadness releases
A boat as fragile as a May butterfly."[2]

This topic cannot be concluded without mentioning the mystic poets who offer their experience through their verses with such an impetus of the "profound" that they can become "breath." Their works are fueled by Love for the Divine, for the absolute. They convey an authentic message of a quest without compromise and can thus show the recipient the "right" Way that can lead him to his essential Being — *at least if...*

The famous "Shin Jin Mei" — *verses on the faith* — of Master Sosan, the most ancient sacred text of Chan, should be mentioned here; *it is exemplary as a working guide and as a witness of a real Awakening.*

---

1. Haïkaï de Basho et de ses disciples, Institut international de coopération intellectuelle, Paris, 1936.

2. Arthur Rimbaud, *Complete works, selected letters*, The University of Chicago Press, 2005, p. 135.

For example,

"The Truth is beyond time and space,
one instant is eternity,
Not here, not there —
but everywhere always right before your eyes."[1]

It is also essential to mention the Sufi teaching, which has often been the bearer of exceptional works, written by unusual Seekers.

There are many, but we will only quote Jalāl ad-Dīn Rūmī, who advocated the use in poetry of intuitive imagery, result of ecstatic spiritual experiences. Here is his experience in two verses which, evoking the encounter with the Other, make one wish to continue further on the path:

"O you, who in me recite this poetry,
I would be disobedient to you if I did not listen to you and repeat."[2]

Often, these mystic artists wrote their works in reaction against the established religious institutions that no longer respected the original messages. One of the most striking examples is undoubtedly Kabir, an illiterate poet — *or a metaphor about the Seeker who has gone beyond words and their limits; this is to say, a rejection of any alienating form* — who lived in Benares in the 15th century. He spoke out against the blinding of man in all areas, including religion, criticizing the misguidedness of both Muslims and Hindus.

"O brother, where do these two masters of the world come from?
Who has turned you away from the right path?
Allah, Ram, Karim, Keshav, Hari, Hazrat:
Who gave them these names?"[3]

Which did not stop both religions from venerating him; the purity of his thought illuminates any person in quest. Through the reading of his work appears a Way of liberation, bare, without con-

---

1. Seng-ts'an (Sosan), *Hsin-Hsin Ming,* interpretation by Eric Putkonen.

2. Rumi, *Le livre du dedans*, Edition Albin Michel, 1997.

3. Yves Moatty, *Kabir: le fils de Ram et d'Allah,* Édition Les deux Océans, 1988.

cession or embellishment, with structure and form disappearing.

To end this topic, two verses of the poet expressing a transcendence — *that echo those of Jalāl ad-Dīn Rūmī:*

> *"Him whom I went out to seek, I found just where I was: He now has become myself whom before I called 'Another!'"*[1]

THE INTERNAL ARTS

Behind the term "internal Art" hides a pleonasm. In fact, any Art is internal because it is an expression of the spiritual accomplishment of man, at least in theory. Nonetheless, in the secular world this notion is so overused that the determinant "internal" has its purpose. Particularly, to differentiate the "internal Arts" from those "external," like: modern yoga, judo, karate, tai chi, qigong, etc., which are often considered as full-fledged sports or fun wellness activities. Also, most of the time, these "arts" are transformed into profitable products *offered* to the public at large. It is enough to observe to confirm this.

The learning of these activities is done in a methodical way, by dissecting them analytically. The posture, the movement, the principle, all are defined and standardized under the pretext of an optimum performance. But obviously, as can be inferred, the training actually corresponds to the educational method used in school. So, no disturbance, no questioning of the received conditioning, everything is in harmony, or almost. Formal and normalized, this teaching is accessible to the largest number of people — *certainly allowing for better sales.*

The showcase of the standard models, the various promotions and in some cases the competition between individuals have become the main references of these "arts." While the federative structures complete the collective alienation.

Be careful, though, it is not at this level that the deceit lies. What

1. Yves Moatty, *Kabir: le fils de Ram et d'Allah,* Édition Les deux Océans, 1988.

we just described is the contemporary world of sport. The activities mentioned are most of the time presented as sports or leisure, so there is no deception. The imposture appears when those "arts" are presented as "disciplines with a spiritual aim" when they actually offer no content whatsoever. For example, "modern" Tai Chi Chuan, which very often details, through the usual attractive discourse, the Chi — *or Qi, nowadays translated as "energy," the modern term for the breath* — and its relation with the Yi — *directed intention*, the Shen — *spirit* —, and the gesture, and ultimately loses its essence as a tool of the "Profound." Its expression is then nothing but a formal search for predefined appearance and feeling, annihilating any interior transmutation — *"Poetry stops at the idea, any idea kills it."*

One can see that translating Chi — or Qi — by using the term "energy," makes it lose its initial meaning of "breath," which is universal: Prana, Pneuma, spiritus, Ruh, Ruah, Ki. But "energy[1]" "speaks" more, "performs" more and thus "sells more."

By the way, there is a rarely mentioned yet fundamental point, which is the difference between the desire "to achieve results" and to "move beyond oneself." To clarify this difference:

When working with the aim of developing one's "inner energy" — *Chi, Ki, Prana, Dan tian, Hara or other* — the spirit can only be "stone" because it is focused on one's small dimension. It is egocentric. How can one reach the infinite, the Tao or the Divine in that case? How can one transcend oneself?

It is the same type of work as "modern" Qigong, detailing the principles, explaining the meridians, researching predefined sensations, determining goals, all for a potential well-being or a molded spirituality...

Predefining an objective molds it and thus formalizes any future experience. The Mind is then imprisoned in a rigid will limited to

1. The origin of this "translation: interpretation" comes without doubt from Bergson, *Spiritual Energy: Essays and Lectures*, 1919 — texts and conferences published between 1901 and 1913. Note: although it was specified as "spiritual energy."

the definition received. As a consequence, the Other cannot awaken. This is why it is said to "want without wanting" and to go toward the undefinable.

The authentic Masters do not explain the "why," they focus on the "how," on the Spirit. The *"energy"* is of no importance, the notion of performance is to be forgotten. One must tend mentally toward the ineffable to create the relation interior / exterior and allow the breath / Spirit to merge with the undivided breath, all while letting go — *a paradox that can only be understood through experience.* This work is of the Nei Kung type — *internal work.* It can allow, if the qualities of the Seeker are present, to access a "right" spiritual work.

The above applies to almost all Far Eastern arts that are commercialized today.

> *To stimulate our imagination, let us take as an example a Yoga practitioner from several centuries ago, practicing day and night to achieve the deliverance of his Soul / Spirit (moksha) through postures (asana), meditation (dhyana), and work with the breath (pranayama), who arrives in our time and sees what the sacred disciplines have become. What would he think?*
>
> *Indeed, commercial products promising a spirituality available to everyone, or other products aimed at well-being or sculpting a perfect body. Without forgetting the recreational associations to fill the time. A sad reality.*
>
> *Of course, as always, exceptions do exist; but they have to be found.*

This is why we speak of "degeneration" in the previous chapter. Many of these Arts become corrupted for the usual reasons, power and money. To obtain those are used either the theories of scholars from ancient China or "pseudosciences" rationalizing the obscure teachings that appear to escape any logic; forgetting in both cases that the work to be done must avoid pure Reason — *the how, the know-how of the Tool is to be prioritized.* To complete the whole, the wearing of uniforms is advocated as a support to the molding of the group.

Many other aberrations exist and the list is very long — *a perfect reflection of the blunders of the different spiritual paths.* A few examples:

- Those who, with a blissful smile, float on a cloud of predefined wisdom displaying the standardized appearance of the awakened Master.
- Others who, thinking themselves the warriors of Far Eastern tales and legends, try to prove their invincibility on submissive opponents.
- Without forgetting the appearance of the posture, the folkloric outfits, the aesthetics of the standardized movements, all with the aim to attract, to have the expected success on the social networks.
- Etc.

Just like in the case of spiritual, religious or initiatory quests, one can only be surprised by the lack of foresight of the Seekers victims of such lures.

The internal Art's "purpose" is not to make the practitioner stand out or render his *inner energy* more performant, but to merge him into the Tao.

Exactly like poetry:

- The internal Art is a tool of accomplishment.
- The internal Art is the result of the accomplishment.

It should be reminded that these *"deviations"* are identical to those of the trendy Far Eastern religions. The internal *energy*, the types of *energy*, the meridians that this *energy* follows are explained. Then, an ersatz of the Buddhist "spirit" and of Taoist "science" is added: the five elements, the three sages, the I Ching — *the book of divination; forgetting that the historical Buddha rejected all forms of divination* —, and sometimes the Chinese pharmacopeia. Syncretism reigns!

Originally, the I Ching presented a certain "simplicity," consequence of the observation of nature, understandable only for the "accomplished person," then increased in complexity in three stages (3000, 1122, 1000 BC), to finally be interpreted by Confucian scholars in the 4th century B.C.[1] — the same errors, yesterday and today.

The packaging is beautiful and attractive, and easily understood by the layman, but the spiritual essence is so diluted that it ends up disappearing.

"Where are the Masters of old?" can only lament the Seeker. "In the shadow," as per the tradition, away from any possible contagion.

The evolution of the Seeker in these Arts may be the following:

The ordinary practitioner will be seeking the means to defend himself or to improve his health. There is no objection to be made here. This is the survival instinct, and therefore a natural tendency.

But it can also be the desire to stand out, either to imitate the Master's archetype, so as to possess the power and privileges linked to the title, or to be the "leader of the pack" through sheer physical force or by instilling fear. Such a person can be attractive, making powerful aesthetic movements, which are also "full." "Full" means that the internal pressure, due either to the neurotendinous or to isometric work, is present. His thrust is effective and his speech interesting. The students call him "Master."

The first step will be the understanding of the Art through Reason. The practitioner discovers that behind the first impression there exists an unexpected world — *or hoped for, depending on the person.* He tries to understand, using logic, which process can generate the anticipated accomplishment. His initial aim remains the same, but he progressively discovers the subtlety of the work to be done, as well as the influence it can have on his Mind.

The second step begins when he realizes that the tools provided allow him to reach a particular state. The gesture leads his Spirit, then, little by little, the Spirit leads the "right" gesture in the learned form. The Spirit becomes more important than the physical.

---

1. Pierre Riffard, *Ésotérismes d'ailleurs*, Éditions Robert Laffont, 1997.

In this way the stillness of the meditation meets the movement and the movement meets the stillness. The "breath" emerges; it is internal and allows to be "pneumatic."

The third step begins when the connection between interior and exterior occurs and the Other appears. Then, the subjective separation of his Being from the All is breached. This breach is a perceptive revelation opening the way toward transcendence.

Masters from different traditions were able to express their experience with words, retracing the steps described. Therefore,

- The Seeker understands through experience how: *"The Spirit must become substance and this substance must become form"* Wang Xiangzhai.
- And consequently everything becomes simpler, the gesture loses its formalism and becomes natural, spontaneous: *"Your Art, when it is natural, will become wonderful"* Guo Yunshen.
- But the following basic principle must be respected: *"One must seek spiritual rightness and not formal exactness"* Wang Xiang Jai.
- In this way, over time, the Art is forgotten and only the Essential remains: *"…and our entire body, our entire soul, will become light"* Morihei Ueshiba.

At this stage the spiritual quest is self-sufficient.

IN CONCLUSION OF THIS CHAPTER

Our objective was to show, using the examples of poetry and the internal Arts, that despite a great difference in terms of expression, these two Ways — *Dao/Tao in Chinese, or Do in Japanese* — could also correspond to authentic spiritual quests.

The same can be said for other Arts, such as dance, sculpture, painting, etc. The works of Van Gogh or Dali would only confirm this. However, the accomplishment of these two artists is not obvious to everyone. Not because of the social and moral judgments that can be made, but because on the spiritual level their radiance was not manifest.

Although, Dali's derision of everything, himself included, seems to indicate a palpable realization, and his whimsical attitude is similar to the Zen metaphor on the meaning of life: *"a great burst of laughter"* — *an image also used in Sufi thought.*

As to Vincent Van Gogh, his life attests to an incessant unfinished quest. Refusing to accept that art can be traded, he tried to take refuge in religion, but in the face of the refusal of the institution he had a chaotic, to say the least, life and a dramatic end; evidence of his inner suffering.

It is possible, as some Masters of the tradition point out, that this is due to too strong of an attachment to the Tool. In fact, once the third stage has begun — *verifiable through the quality of their works* — the tool, painting, becomes a burden, a stifling attachment. The tool, then, would supplant the Work — *their own accomplishment.*

Paradoxically, some Seekers have succeeded in sublimating their art, thus giving way to a completed spiritual Path. One example is the accomplished Master of the internal, Morihei Ueshiba, founder of Aikido, who managed to transform a martial method into a true Art. About which he said:

"When you bow deeply to the universe, it bows back; when you call

out the name of God, it echoes inside you.[1] "

This is reminiscent of the verses of the mystic poets mentioned previously; the paths are many, but the "impetus" that underlies the quest is the same.

Unfortunately, it is easy to see that the content of these messages of quality is very often corrupted and serves limited ends. The societal *evolution* is undoubtedly at the origin of this degeneration, or maybe it would be better to say:

"People rarely have the qualities required to understand the transmitted message."

1. Morihei Ueshiba, John Stevens, *The Art of Peace*, Shambhala Publications, 2005, p. 181.

EVERYDAY LIFE AS
OPERATIVE WORK

Numerous books have dealt with the present topic, repeating over and over the theories shared by most of the trending teachings. The materials used are most often extracted from the Far Eastern traditions — *India, Tibet, Japan, China* — while preserving the enchanting aspect of the popular images describing them.

Regarding the application of the principles to remember, most of the time it is explained that each daily act has to become exercise. For that to happen, it is advised to be present at every moment, to open one's senses so as to be fully in the "present moment," or to be "fully aware" of the "here and now" — *today's misleading terms.*

By the way, this fashion of mindfulness, allowing not to be troubled by one's thoughts, has always made the authentic traditions smile. This is the "stubborn emptiness" of Chan, which can also be translated as: "mindfulness, yes, and then what?"

But what is forgotten here is that such an approach is only a first step. It is about concentration, the basic principle of any work on oneself, be it arts, sports, driving, or any learning in general. However, trying to define it as an exercise that must be done every day and every moment is an aberration.

Let us explain this assertion.

Those who have practiced know that it is extremely difficult to be in a vigilant state — *"present moment," "here and now," "mindfulness"* — during a defined exercise and in optimal conditions of calmness, and this without a "mental opening[1]." Therefore, in the family environment, at work or when commuting, where the conditions are often disruptive or even stressful, this becomes almost impossible.

It would be better, "in the beginning" and for a very long time, to work only with the tools transmitted on a daily basis and with pleasure, as if it were a "refuge," a haven of peace — *with time and experience this will indeed become the case.*

As always, words have their limits. To better understand this idea of "refuge," a few examples of experiences that most of us have lived would be of help. It must be said beforehand that this is the type of perception felt only when one is in perfect symbiosis with one's environment.

This can happen in the countryside, in the mountains or at the sea. You are alone, in front of an exceptional sight that only nature can offer: a sunrise, a storm in the mountains, an infinite expanse of water with a soft breeze, etc. Submerged in this harmony, the weight of the mask, of the Persona, disappears. You are "naked" in front of the surrounding "Universe." There is no judgment, no aggression, you can relax, unwind and forget yourself.

It is this mental relaxation that is the backbone of all work, of any quest. It melts the "stone" part of the Spirit, which becomes supple, soft like a breeze, in one word "breath."

The breath is able to move inside the body because of its lightness and subtleness, it can join not only the exterior, but also the All, the Divine, the Tao. From that moment on, everything comes together, the tree, the stream, even the sound becomes "palpable" like the air, like the sun, like the earth.

It is also the feeling of becoming a fetus once again and joining the universal matrix. The one that loves us and that can only accept us.

It is the state of meditation, of prayer, of mantra.

1. A mental opening is the moment when the concentration on a subject disappears, masked by a disruptive thought or a different, distracting perception.

This state remains exceptional and to think that it can be achieved continually in everyday life, following some reading and a few seminars, is a "sweet" lie.

On the other hand, if you do make sure to be present as much as possible in most of your acts, the exercise will bring about some surprises. Indeed, it is good to know that, because of this willingness to be present, the mind is taken by the deliberate attention and the unexpected consequence is that every action becomes clumsy. As previously mentioned, concentration is the first step in any learning. You may recall how, when you were driving for the first time, you had to pay attention to every decision and every gesture, with your cortex slowing you down. Only the intuitive knowledge afterwards, when the gesture is forgotten, allowed you to become free and fluid.

This first stage is conscious will and it is clumsy.

It is the state of concentration.

As explained in another book, Abraham Maslow's learning progression in four stages can be used as a reference here. 1- I do not know that I do not know, 2- I know that I do not know, 3- I know that I know, 4- I do not know that I know. The stage of concentration corresponds to the 3rd stage of Maslow's progression.

Over time, thanks to the application of the principles mentioned, working with the Tool will progressively modify one's field of consciousness. The next step can begin. It is conscious presence, where one is in the act without effort of the "stone" will; this is a difficult to understand paradox for the layman, who is "conscious of the *presence* and in parallel is in the useful reflective."

Once arrived at this stage, one paradox has to be addressed — the desire to be present in "full awareness" and its so-called opposition with thought. We must not delude ourselves, in working life we have no choice but to use our reflective thinking on the professional level to analyze the "interconnections" of acts and decisions; which is just as true in family life. The "empty" mind, the famous emptiness, is not the rejection of such types of indispensable mental activity, but rather the cessation of "uncontrolled" thoughts — not to be confused with the unconscious, which can provide very useful information. As a reminder, the non-thought without perception of the presence inside oneself — "breath / Spirit" — in Chan Buddhism is called "stubborn emptiness"...

This presence stems from one's center, it is nimble.

This is the state of active mediation.

Then one day, one moment, a perfect harmony is created between oneself and the whole; a bright moment of simplicity and well-being. The "right" gesture is made in the simplest way possible. One is in tune with everything and moves without wanting, without the "I" which slowly fades away; it is union with the essential Being. Any theory pales in comparison with this burst of light.

The presence, inside and outside oneself, is subtle and universal.

This is the state of active contemplation — so, the three stages described: concentration, meditation, contemplation.

It is easy to see that the first stage, that of concentration, pales in comparison to the other two. Nevertheless, it must be remembered that any work on oneself is, in the beginning and for a long time afterwards, extremely difficult.

The difficulty comes from our Reason, which is continuously, at every moment, autonomous. It speculates incessantly on anything but what we are actually doing. It spins left and right, changes direction, only to continue further.

And if one follows the usual advices on non-thought — *thoughts are clouds that roll by and one must not focus on any of them; or, burning thoughts in a fire* — Reason, by its gift of ubiquity, still deceives us. Reason is the will to stop the speculative state and the reflective thinking itself, both becoming exponential.

So how to concentrate?

The usual notion of will must be forgotten in the practical action that is to be taken, knowing that it will still be there. The "secret" is relaxation, "letting go" with the principal aim of "losing one's restlessness." It is this restlessness that causes our misalignment with the Other.

Relaxation, letting go, alignment of the mind with the action to be performed.

Any willingness to act too urgently or too willingly, sign of the apprentice, gives rise to clumsy tension and, above all, to mental restlessness. One must calm the mind by becoming an observer, by relativizing any and all objectives, and by relaxing.

The alignment of body and mind will happen progressively.

> *This is why any objective is wrong, be it spiritual — awakening, health-promoting — energy, Qi, Ki, or other. Only the change of state of Being and later Soul is "right." It is necessary to tend toward the "impetus of the profound" which does not care about any success or any concrete result. The authentic Masters of Taoism say: "there is nothing to look for because there is nothing to be found"...*

The work to be carried out every day is also connected to the improvement of one's human qualities, which is also essential to any initiatory path. This will allow you to transcend the tool and in turn to transcend yourself.

> *A scientific study by Doctor Masaru Emoto[1] proved through observation that — frozen — water crystals can be influenced, not only by the material environment — music, place —, but also by immaterial thought — prayer, mantra, mediation. Depending on the situation, these crystals may have a harmonious and balanced structure or be completely tortured.*
>
> *This phenomenon tends to confirm our initial assertion: the tool you are going to use will be useful for your accomplishment, but you yourself must have the required qualities so as to perform productive work.*
>
> *A very subtle synergy!*

1. Masaru Emoto, *The Hidden Messages in Water*, Beyond words publishing company, 2004.

What good is it to punctually develop your relationship with your Soul-Spirit through mantras and prayers if the rest of the time you are small, petty, envious or hateful?

Not only will the tool not create anything beneficial to you, but in addition your Spirit will be sullied by your thoughts and behavior. Your own accomplishment will become impossible, except maybe for the dark work, but your petty side will still be an impediment — *we will not go further in this deviation.*

So, open your Mind toward the Good in your everyday life. Not the Good, moral of the society, but the one from your personal ethics, linked to your compassion and empathy. This sensitivity which makes you act for the other, not to receive something beneficial in return, not because of some superstition to avoid misfortune, not to stand out, but because deep inside yourself you feel the need to act this way.

If for the moment this is not the case, simply follow the moral precepts of your initiatory school. Also, surround yourself with people of quality and, slowly, like the water crystals, your personal quality will improve.

Over time you will notice that deep inside you there is a truth of the Good. A truth not of the dogma, but of the Heart, "Love-unity."

Obviously, you should not think you are invested by God, which would only give you a new mask. Instead, you should accept yourself as you are, with a relative love, not yet and maybe never universal, but fundamentally free for those most deprived. This improvement of your qualities should lead you to *"think good, say good, do good."* One day you will understand concretely that Saint Augustine was right when he said:

"*To deceive by the Spirit is already to deceive.*"

Remain in a modest dimension, that of any human Being. Do not constantly ask for the "impossible," which will last only for a short time — *soon to be covered by a deceptive mask —*, but "strive for the ideal as often as possible."

This is the main thing. The impetus inside oneself, the one driving you without any logical or speculative reason, the one giving you the strength to persevere in spite of your problems and limitations, the one that is "life" and cannot be measured. Whether it starts from the "lowest" level of the individual or the "highest" one, it still is an impetus. It is a state of Soul par excellence. And on this level, any measurement is wrong.

Many are discouraged from the beginning, thinking that they do not have the intelligence, the Awakening, the necessary virtues, or discovering along the way that they are not who they thought they were. But none of these are important, only the "spiritual impetus" is fundamental.

And it must always be remembered that even if previously one was not in accordance with the principles mentioned, the past cannot be changed, but the future can be what one decides it to be. People should stop believing that the Awakening, the discovery of the "Other," the Tao, the encounter with the Light or the Divine, are accessible only to a predefined elite.

We wrote this essay in part for this reason.

Too many speakers and representatives of various religions or initiatory schools would have us believe, with the complexity of their explanations and the flaunting of their culture, that only those who have such abilities can access a dimension qualified as superior.

While, on the contrary, it is often the simplest people who are most sensitive to the spiritual dimension — *on the condition, of course, that the initial conditioning does not have too strong a grip on them.*

This reminds the words of Jesus:

"Blessed are the poor in spirit, for theirs is the kingdom of heaven." —Matthew 5:3

"Let the little children come to me, and do not hinder them, for the kingdom of heaven belongs to such as these." —Matthew 19:14

It should be noted that "simple" or "child" does not mean, in this case, to be ignorant or stupid, but a state of soul regained, a state of simplicity and sensitivity.

"Among those born of women, from Adam until John the Baptist, there is no one so superior to John the Baptist that his eyes should not be lowered (before him). Yet I have said, whichever one of you comes to be a child will be acquainted with the kingdom and will become superior to John." —*Gospel of Thomas 46*
Which can also be found in Lao-Tzu's —*Tao Te King:*
"He who displays himself does not shine." —*Tao Te King 24*
"So it is that some things are increased by being diminished, and others are diminished by being increased." —*Tao Te King 42*
Or, in the Buddhist vows:
"Wear no jewelry or other adornments, use no perfume whatsoever."

Remember that: "You are as you are, as nature, God, has made you." Trust your abilities, they have been put in every human. Study and learn, the experience of others is always useful. But do not nurture the sophistication of everything, this will only render it opaque and will in fact hinder any "right" vision. This simplicity to be sought is the basis of Being and not of Semblance.

In everyday life:

-   Rid yourself of the cloak of your Persona, let yourself be carried by your "nature" — *while keeping an eye on the animal inside you, if this is still necessary* — and, as much as possible, keep an inner smile.

-   Do not distort your inner expression with borrowed words, which will create an illusory appearance, and thus put on another new cloak.

-   Do not seek the appearance that will make you stand out or differentiate you, be it an improvised look or the rejection of the societal uniform. The uniform is uniform and non-uniform. It is by rejecting the "common uniform" that some people make themselves stand out, without realizing that they are putting on a new uniform, that of the asocial, of the awakened, of the master, of the initiated, etc. The abstraction of oneself begins with an ordinary appearance — *something many so-called masters of wisdom seem to have forgotten.*

Another essential part of the "everyday life as work" is the "work of observation," which must be constant. This may seem simple, but it is in fact much more difficult than what one may think.

Of course, it consists "only" in observing.

Observing the others, but also the observer, oneself.

In some Far Eastern schools, one is advised to place one's attention at the same time in one's vision and, in parallel, on a specific point of the brain. Other schools teach to look without attachment at what is being observed and others yet to look beyond the things observed, as if looking at the horizon.

Whatever the method chosen, it is advisable, as always, to forget any theory, while preserving the principle used.

Furthermore, an important point so that these precepts can be applied: it consists in "taking a step back" from the situation lived, but while being present at the level of perception. This perspective is mainly at the level of your emotional agitation.

To clarify, emotional agitation is the consequence of an emotion, whatever it may be, which creates mental agitation and often a — *unrealized* — psychological and physical impulse.

As a consequence, there are three possible intuitive reactions — aggression, flight, inhibition.

To take this step back, observe your emotions and above all avoid resorting to any stereotype definitions relating to "premature Awakening," that is, putting on the "mask of the Sage" when trying to detach oneself from emotions — *in other words, a new mask of "non-attachment."*

Your emotions are part of the human nature, let them express themselves. In some situations they are very useful, in others not so much. But even in the latter cases, accept the following impulses without suffering them; this will allow you to be aware of them without being their unknowing victim.

As a side note, if you believe that you can detach yourself from your emotional reactions, you are deluding yourself.

An authentic Chan Master — there are few of them, a euphemism — used to put a plastic bag on the head of those who claimed to be emotionally detached, even in the presence of mortal danger. And when these "pseudo-sages of the insensitive" had begun to suffocate, all without exception struggled, panic-stricken, to remove the bag, and the Master laughed.

The fact of rejecting an emotion only hides it from your reason, but it will still have an effect at the level of the deep brains. Consequently, there will be mental blockage.

Fear, for example, exists even in the greatest champions of combat sports. They know it and they do not reject it, and thanks to that they do not suffer it; they are not frozen by it; and they even use it sometimes.

So, do the same, use your emotions and senses to feel "the real from the fake" in you and in others. Be simple, do not distort reality.

Over time, you will realize that most people play a role. They are children seeking shelter behind their societal and familial role. They put on the uniform / mask of the professor, doctor, soldier, artisan, priest, intellectual, father, mother, responsible, etc. Some are convinced of their role, others a little less so. Sometimes there is doubt. There are unexpressed laughs, cries, joy, heartache and fear. And they are not alone, you will discover that it is the same for you.

This *partial* discovery of the mask is often traumatizing.

One then sees what one had hidden from oneself, what one did not want to see: one's weaknesses and small-mindedness.

Few can bear this realization.

It is at this moment that Reason uses a new subterfuge to stop the quest of the Seeker. A very effective one, found in the following questions:

- "This is not the right path,"
- Or "The tool is bad and incomplete,"
- And most of the time, the Koan question par excellence: "What is the point?"

Some Seekers end their quest at this point and join "those who are crazy without being so."

There is a way to avoid this pitfall though.

When you observe, do not judge, but rather try to make fun of that which you consider to be an illusion and of no great interest — *which was one of the most remarkable abilities of Zen monks of quality.*

Thanks to this derision, you will be able to avoid certain excesses without making a judgment of "good or bad," a dualism which can only make you regress. You will also be able to smile at yourself and accept what you discover — *which does not mean that subsequently you should not look to improve yourself, the advantage here is that this allows you to become aware of your "stage performance."*

You must observe as if your fellow men were children. However, you should oppose with all your strength any evil act or any hateful individual carrying the evil inside him — *a paradox resulting from the impetus that "opens" your sensitive perception and not based on moral analysis.*

All of this, with time, will help you to relax.

The others are like you, with their stupidity, their intelligence, their certainties, their doubts, their roles, their naivety, their pettiness, their generosity, their goodness, their mediocrity, their greatness, their baseness, their rigidity and their questionings. The only difference, and it is a big one, is that you are aware of it and this allows you to open yourself.

You can tell a loved one or yourself: "I am suffering, I am in pain" without a false sense of shame.

You can tell a loved one or yourself: "Your action is blameworthy, your mind is going astray" without hate or resentment.

This will remove a large burden from your shoulders.

And you can slip away from the vague desperate agitation that surrounds you.

Work like this, day after day, and you will advance on the path of your quest,

And the Impetus will carry you!

REASON AND SPIRIT

Before concluding, we thought it useful to do an overview of the respective roles of "Reason" and "Spirit[1]," the latter being a cornerstone in any spiritual quest — *this chapter will be a condensed overview of what was discussed until here.*

To begin with, let us define what is Reason and what is Spirit. Useful definitions, because nowadays there is a complete confusion among most people as to how these two "faculties" should be understood. A confusion maintained by our "Knowledgeables."

Who do we mean by "Knowledgeables"?

Certainly not the thinkers and philosophers who stood or are standing against the frozen institution and against codified religion, and who side with the interests of man in society.

Nor the engineers, doctors and professors who work to improve the living conditions of people.

"Knowledgeables" are those who, satisfied with their acquired culture and knowledge, approach everything, even the spiritual, through discursive analysis, through speculation and logic based on

---

1. In the text:
   - Spirit, spiritus: "the corporeal / incorporeal substance" linking man to the Divine, to the Tao, to the universe — not to be confused with the Soul.
   - Not to be confused with *mind*: usually used to describe the principles of the psyche, the intellectual and affective faculties and sometimes the way of being.
   - Reason: all intellectual faculties, discerning true from false and good from bad, as well as organizing the relation with the real.
   - Soul: transcendent principle of man, but also "pure individualized consciousness" or "sensitive perception" and not individuation, personality or persona; it can be the link of consciousness between the "corporeal substance" and the "incorporeal substance," or "Soul / Spirit."

the intellect, thus rejecting the sensitive and perceptive approach of the Spirit.

They reduce the chaotic and irrational dimension of the Spirit to a vague pseudo-elitist theory, understandable only by a minority who thinks itself "chosen."

In contemporary society, the Knowledgeables are "The" reference of "right-thinking." They control the thoughts of the "common man" who can only see a single approach to the realm of the Spirit — *religious, initiatory or artistic* —, the one using Reason.

While obvious, this is never mentioned because it is demonstrated, by its conceptual logic, that Reason guides the Spirit and this is proven beyond doubt using discursive analysis — *product of said Reason*. And in consequence, those who dare doubt this assertion find themselves accused of ignorance and stupidity.

In addition, and this should not be forgotten, the worlds of literature, art and religion are in the hands of these "Knowledgeables"; they are uncontested references of the media because they are incontestable — *because of the societal conditioning of the individual.*

A closed and fixed system that is not ready to change, despite the awareness of our society, which notices the loss of its spirituality, without realizing that it itself has caused it. But everything is cyclical…

In 1864, the historian Fustel de Coulanges already observed that:
"The word religion did not signify what it signifies for us; by this word we understand a body of dogmas, a doctrine concerning God, a symbol of faith concerning what is in and around us. This same word, among the ancients, signified rites, ceremonies, acts of exterior worship. The doctrine was of small account: the practices were the important part; these were obligatory, and bound man (ligare, religio).[1]"

This confusion appears constantly and it is not surprising to see it develop rapidly in any spiritual "novelty" introduced in the West. An initiatory tradition, a new Art appears, initially transmitted as

---

1. Numa Denis Fustel de Coulanges, *The ancient city*, Dover publications, 2006, p. 167.

is customary, from Master to disciple, to a very small number of people, discreetly or even secretly, with work on the Spirit using ancestral tools the knowledge of which was empirical. What becomes of it?

Immediately, a few specialists of "our sciences" seize it, develop its understanding through analysis, rationalize its tools and define the standard model of the practitioner, as well as the goal to be met. Then, based on these definitions, they develop an institution, a structured federation to better control the practitioners, all while advertising it to attract people.

A very negative vision, one may say, but realistic if one is willing to open one's eyes, or rather Heart.

This does not mean, of course, that it is a good idea to reject Reason, which has made it possible to put in place the elements of a certain well-being, as well as to define the moral and social laws central to any society.

Moreover, it can be argued that, exceptionally, working with Reason can allow access to the Spirit, at least if one respects, according to the original tradition, an initiatory logic, and above all if one combines it with regular work on the sensitive and the perceptive; work which can only be very, very, long...

This is the key point to be remembered. The passage from Reason to Spirit must occur, otherwise there can only be stagnation, if not even regression. There is no opposition between Reason and Spirit, which can, only at a specific moment, fuse together. It is possible to think that it is from this fusion that the moral precepts of the "religious archetypes" have originated and which have allowed our society to free itself, to a greater or lesser extent, from animality.

Now that we have described the existing confusion, let us look at the two notions and reveal the real difference between them.

Reason is the faculty to think and judge according to one's intellect. Through logic, analysis and predefined parameters, it allows us to establish a judgment on one or a set of phenomena, or to speculate on their consequences — *in other words, to project oneself into the future or into the theory.*

We are not talking about the "transcendent intellect" — *intuitive cognizance* — of Aristotle which is Reason and Spirit — *the aim* —, but about the "discursive mind," the cortex. Also should be excluded the "traditional Hindu or Chinese Logic" which induces the assimilation of the essence of the object by the subject and which thus takes a different dimension since it is intuitive, if not spiritual, because the relation between subject and object is taken as a whole — *in its Unity.* It thus goes beyond that Reason which limits the object to the learned and recorded definition, without taking into account the variable resulting from the perceptive relation — *except when the subject is aware of the sensitive link uniting everything, subject and object merging together; but this is almost the culmination, and thus the exception* — as the poet said: "inanimate object, do you have a soul...?". A "variable" that disappears from the perception of the common man and who consequently builds his individuation.

> *Paul D. MacLean specifies in his triune brain theory that the cortex also has the function of separating consciously man from his environment[1]. One can thus better understand the difficulty of the path to be followed.*

This is the consequence of the education received by the subject from childhood; which is true today both in the Far East and in the West. An education based on formal and rigid knowledge, built on the limited definition of everything, on dualism and differentiation. Data which could have been constructive if evolving, but which is paralyzing because of its immutability.

This last point may seem obscure to the reader, so we will explain it in detail.

The definition of an object[2] puts it in a defined set according to parameters established on references such as form, size, color,

---

1. Paul D. MacLean, *The Triune Brain in Evolution: Role in Paleocerebral Functions,* Plenum, 1990.

2. Object: anything, animate or inanimate, that affects the senses.

function, composition, etc. These parameters thus particularize the object, delimit it, and above all limit the perceptive of the subject. Therefore they limit the Reason and cut it from the Spirit.

In fact, the subject can have a perception that is completely different from the imposed definition, but cannot communicate it to the Reason because of his conditioning, hence the subjective rupture between the conscious and the unconscious.

What is more, the definition of everything is based on dualist criteria: big, small, black, white, soft, hard, good, bad, etc.

Therefore, a Reason is constructed that works on the binary level, like a computer, and it limits the Spirit or at least the conscious perception. As an obvious consequence, the contemporary man, proud and satisfied with his intellectual achievement, limits the spirit of the "Anthropopithecus[1]" that we are to the realm of Reason and the Universe to the definition.

By the way, to be more explicit, let us look at the initiatory schools trying to get their members out of the rut of the definition by using the symbol. The symbol allows the person working on its multiple meanings to understand that its interpretation is infinite if not indefinite — *knowing that the so-called natural link between the signifier and the signified can vary according to the quality of the interpreter.*

> *This is why, as with any spiritual approach, Christianity, Buddhism, Taoism, Islam or other, it is better to say the Indefinable or the Inexpressible, words leaving open a definition that cannot be one.*
>
> *This can be found in: "Master, my mouth is wholly incapable of saying whom you are like." —Gospel of Thomas 13*
>
> *Or, in the assertion of the Prior of Mont des Cats abbey: "To define God is to distance oneself from Him!"*
>
> *As for Taoism:*

1. The term "Anthropopithecus," "an ape with the characteristics of a human," is used on purpose; the term (Homo) Sapiens, "intelligent, wise, discerning, judicious," does not seem appropriate for the common man.

> *"The Tao that can be trodden is not the enduring and unchanging Tao." —Tao Te King 1*
> *"The Tao, considered as unchanging, has no name." —Tao Te King 32*
> *"The Tao is hidden, and has no name." —Tao Te King 41*
> And Islam:
> *"God is without form or attributes, unknowable and ineffable…"*

This work on the symbol can be considered as the introduction to the "sensitive awakening" of the individual. As previously mentioned, the idea is to get out of the rut of the definition of the object, that is to say of everything — *and not only of the symbol* — at least in theory.

Thus, the "object" can be, "depending on the subject," multiple. This point must be emphasized — "depending on the subject." Because if the subject realizes that the object can vary according to his interpretation, the interpretation can also vary according to the subject.

Obvious, of course, but this should raise a new question so as not to remain in a unidirectional perspective:

- "How can the subject transcend himself and join the infinite of the object?
- Which can be translated as:
- "How can the subject become aware of his multiplicity in order to know that of the object?"

Or:

- "How can the subject join the object?" which implies "How can the subject join the Unity?"

Or, in other words:

- "How to become aware of the Unity?"

And this:

- According to the level of the subject's field of consciousness.

> *To quote Merleau-Ponty: "The miracle of consciousness is to make phenomena appear through attention that reestablish the object's unity in a new dimension at the very moment they destroy that unity."*[1]

And, in this realm, relying only on the speculative approach is deluding oneself.

Because, as previously said, this type of approach is limited to analysis, definition, logic, Reason.

While Unity, the indivisible, or the Divine if you prefer, can only be reached by the "Other," the non-limited perceptive, or in one word the Spirit, because it is without comprehension, without legibility.

One might also wonder if Western philosophy had not taken the wrong path when Saint Thomas Aquinas — *after the Islamic world* — used Aristotle's work to establish the foundation of Christian and scholastic thought. With the axiom of the notion of the subject, variable or not, understood as a conscious entity separate from the object, whatever it might be.

This is what can be considered as an intellectual dimension of man centered on his ego.

> *This is reminiscent of the closed, finite and hierarchical world of Aristotle, who placed earth at the center, fixed and immobile, of the sublunar world — the certain — and of the supra-lunar world — the uncertain —, in other words, the Universe — taken up again by scholastic education with man considered as the center of the Universe.*
>
> *Ego, when you hold us!*

On the contrary, the principle of the possible union between subject and object would have enabled us to reach the notion of wholeness, or even Unicity through the abstraction of the Ego; so, a spiritual dimension.

---

1. Maurice Merleau-Ponty, *Phenomenology of perception*, Routledge, 2012, p.33.

Had Western scholastic education retained this last definition, the notion of God in the Christian world would have been entirely different, although maybe inaccessible to the common man. This is evidenced by the worship of Holinesses, Saints, places, relics, etc. Behavior that can be found in the Far East toward Buddha, considered as a divine entity, in complete opposition with the original message — attitude reproduced by some Westerners, amateurs of Far Eastern traditions, toward divinities, sacred places, relics, Gurus, Tulkus, etc.

Let us look at some of the products of Reason, for example.

Firstly, modern philosophy, defined as "the science of wisdom." The learning of philosophy is done by studying the texts of previous philosophers and by developing the interpretation of said texts — *we find here, once again, the religious education of the "scholastic kind" based on the exegetical study of texts selected by the authorities; which is true for Christians, Muslims or Buddhists.*

It should be noted that the wisdom of ancient Greece had as its foundation the careful observation of nature — and thus the link between it and man — and contemplation; therefore, it was based on the relation between Reason and Spirit.

As an example, the Logos, most often translated as "the Word," actually has another meaning that is often forgotten — because it is too abstract for the speculative mind —, corresponding to the affective part of reason, or "the reason of the heart that produces the intention."

Contemporary philosophy is useful to both the individual and society — *same as static religion.* It establishes, among other things, the definitions of thoughts whose aim is to allow society to live in good harmony. It puts in place a definition of the social Wisdom. It is a reflection on the world.

Another example is psychology, the science of behavior and mental processes. It is supposed to allow to understand the mind by defining the mental processes, while "forgetting" the interdependence with the non-defined, the Unity.

Of course, it is not possible to talk about psychology without mentioning psychoanalysis, the method of analysis of the deep mental processes, or the psyche. There is very often an amalgamation between the psyche and the spiritual.

It can be said that working with Reason develops the psyche of the individual, while work on the Spirit reduces said psyche to make space for the spiritual. As for the tradition, it places the psyche on an intermediary level between Reason and Spirit.

> *Paul opposed the spiritual man — pneumatikos —, to the worldly-minded — psuchikos — who does not possess the Spirit: "But the worldly-minded person does not receive the things of the spirit of God, for they are foolishness to him, and he is not able to know them, because they are spiritually discerned." —1 Corinthians*
>
> *Gnostic Christians have also used this distinction between "hylics" — matter —, "psychics" — mental — and "pneumatics" — Spirit.*
>
> *Which also reminds Lao-Tzu's words:*
>
> *"Scholars of the lowest class, when they have heard about it, laugh greatly at it. If it were not (thus) laughed at, it would not be fit to be the Tao." —Tao Te King 41*

These are just two examples of how work on the Spirit can be confused. The Spirit, however, is at the same time the most intimate and the most common part of the individual. Intimate, because it is deep inside everyone, and common, because it allows to connect with everything, Beings, Divine, Tao. A paradox that can only be understood through experience.

If we take MacLean's theory of the triune brain to illustrate "our conscious relationship with the Spirit," we could situate it at the level of the paleo-mammalian or at the level of the reptilian brain — *that leaves the neomammalian: Reason.*

Why do we place it there?

Because, in the same way that the neomammalian brain cannot control the other two, our conscious will does not have any hold on the Spirit.

We invite you to refer to the specialized publications that deal scientifically with the "triune brain theory" of Doctor MacLean, which is not our topic. However, the following observation is of interest:

"Describing his thoughts (…) he said: 'Each time this thing happens, these thoughts occur very clear and bright to me. They seem as if 'this is what the world is all about — this is the absolute truth.' [1] *"*

"(…) the limbic cortex has the capacity to generate free-floating, affective feelings conveying a sense of what is real, true, and important." [2]

You may want to have Faith, to join the Divine, to merge into the Tao, to be Awakened or to simply improve yourself, you may take on the superficial appearance, but achieving the state will be impossible.

This is where the confusion often lies.

In reality, most specialists of the sciences previously described have the culture and the dialectic required for the theoretical development of religious — *or philosophical* — doctrines, and so, following simple Cartesian logic, they make themselves the mouthpieces for those.

Of course, they do it by using the competence of their Reason, established on the Definition. The obvious consequence is that the layman, finding there the references of his education, understands and assimilates the discourse and texts, and cannot but accept the message transmitted.

Which would not be an issue if the so-called specialists had the willingness — *or the awareness* — to admit their inability to transmit the tools that would allow the spiritual accomplishment of the seeking layman.

Unfortunately, this is not the case, and this teaching is transmitted in a speculative manner, as a "product of the work of Reason," but is paradoxically described as a spiritual achievement.

---

1. Paul D. MacLean, *The Triune Brain in Evolution: Role in Paleocerebral Functions,* Plenum press, 1990, p. 449.

2. Ibid, p. 17

Thus confusion is maintained between:

- Knowledge of the history, rites and texts of the various teachings studied through logical and rhetorical methods, with stereotyped images as a background,
- And the "right" work, through the use of the tools of these teachings, by means of the qualities required by the Tradition.

It must be remembered that a large majority of today's writings on Far Eastern traditions is written by Knowledgeables, who can often be found as opinion leaders of trendy spirituality but rarely as diligent practitioners of the traditional tools — *by diligent we mean tens of years of practice several hours a day.*

Catholicism had had the wisdom of separating these two approaches by creating theology and thus avoiding the confusion — *or almost, because the hierarchical structure put in place can maintain the confusion in the layman.*

Everyone or almost everyone knows the difference between theology and Faith, but few are able to distinguish a philosophical approach from a spiritual quest.

In conclusion of this chapter.

It is essential for any Seeker to become aware of this distinction between Reason and Spirit before undertaking any esoteric steps, so as to be able to distinguish the superficial from the essential throughout his quest.

The "Essential" is confirmed during the initiation to the "right" work with the tools of an authentic tradition. And all authentic traditions work with the same principles — *even if the tools seem different.*

That is:

- To animate the "divided breath" — *also translated as presence of God* — so as to cut the speculative mind — *Reason* —, so that the "essential Being" can progressively emerge — *or, exceptionally, instantly.*

It is this "inner Master" that will allow you to naturally connect with the All, the Tao, the Divine — *the undivided breath*. Union — *then fusion* —, which cannot be realized through the action of the *voluntary brain* — *pure Reason* — alone.

The accomplishment of the Seeker is linked to the proper use of the tools. This will make the "breath, Spirit/Soul" become consciously "perceptible" and thus will allow to gradually take the most important steps. Each step will require the evolution of the principles to be used, which is related to the "openings of the field of consciousness" of the Seeker. But the path is certainly long, very long, if not endless.

The "breath" in question was part of the liturgical vocabulary until the 4th century. The vocabulary distinguished between the "Soul breath" and the "Soul Spirit," a provisional separation that must lead to Unity.

> There is a big confusion between Soul and Spirit.
> The Soul is a person, an animal enjoying life — if we take the Bible as a reference: "Nephesh" in Hebrew, "Psukhe" in Greek, both signifying life as a creature.
> The Soul, obviously, is not the body — "Basar" in Hebrew, "Soma" in Greek: flesh.
> The Spirit indicates either the vital force of the Soul, the universal life principle — "ruah" or "neshama" in Hebrew, "pneuma" in Greek —, or the spiritual life principle, which allows man to connect to God, to the Divine.
> Before the 4th century, they separated the Soul anima — the inspiration and expiration principle of the breath, often badly translated as air: "God blew into his nostrils the breath of life" —from the Soul animus — principle and residence of desires and passions —, which was later replaced by Spiritus. The current confusion is undoubtedly a consequence of some intent or a lack of understanding of the universal breath — which can lead to the divine spirit.

This notion is present in all traditions, be it Jewish, Greek, Latin, Celt, Indian, Chinese or Arabic. It is the product of the traditional tools from around the world — *the list is non-exhaustive*:

- West: meditation, contemplation, prayer, litanies, liturgical chants.
- East: meditation, prayer, Quran verses, Dhikr, Qawwali.
- Far East: meditation, prayer, mantra, Dbyang, shi sheng.

Knowing that the fundamental work with these tools is identical — *when one knows a tradition, the essence of others and the quality of their practitioners are "recognized."*

Which tends to prove the universality of the principles applied, and that the Spirit of man is asleep, whether he is from the East or the West, white, yellow, black or red, poor or rich, learned or not, woman or man.

A divine justice that seems to favor the young child...

CONCLUSION

As you saw in the preceding chapters, contrary to what is most often described, a spiritual quest is not superficial work with the aim to add, layer after layer, new data and new information, while scrupulously respecting unquestionable truths. In fact, it is exactly the opposite, simplicity must be the reference, because it offers the possibility to access one's "essential Being," that "Other" who seems inaccessible to the common man. A multifaceted simplicity to peel off our conditioning, our egocentrism, without forgetting our animal nature, and opening our Spirit to any possibility toward the indefinite.

The Hindu allegory of the onion, saying that to access one's "diamond heart" one must first peel the skins that cover it, is a very revealing image of the "right" spiritual quest.

Jesus illustrates the same essential principle with different words: "But the true circumcision in the Spirit has proved useful in every way." —Gospel of Thomas 53

A spiritual quest is also not about bending one's entire Being to a specific doctrine or ceaselessly navigating between the different "models" offered, based on their attractiveness or how rewarding they are. It should be remembered that the "initial Guides" of today's most important spiritual teachings were opposed to the religious structures of their times, finding them too entrenched to allow any spiritual blossoming — *which does not mean that these teachings are of no interest, but that the formalization of the transmitted messages makes them lose their essence.*

We can quote, as examples, Jesus, who stood against the conservative priestly powers, and Buddha, who questioned the foundations of Hinduism. Obviously, it is not a good idea to compare oneself to these "divine archetypes," however the impetus that guided them can serve as an example.

Hence, it seems salutary to revolt against the merchants of the temple, against the paralyzed and paralyzing institutions, against the ambient conditioning, against the parlor philosophers and boudoir intellectuals, and against the carriers of denatured religions.

For that it seems useful to at least:
- Not play any role on the path of our quest; we should avoid wearing the attires of the Saint, the Blessed one, the Awakened one or the Chosen one,
- Not limit the quest to borders predefined by the dogmas of the different teachings or their governing structures.
- Not give in to the temptation to become a clone of "perfection" and see oneself transformed into a pale copy of the sage, sanitized and without taste,
- Let oneself be carried by intuition, which will be the guarantor of one's experience, after, of course, having washed the stains that could tarnish it.
- Open one's Heart — *Heart/Spirit* — and listen to it.
- Not hesitate to be strong, to be weak, to love, to reject, to give, to receive, to suffer, to be happy, or in other words, to communicate with others, with the "Other," with the All, the Tao, the Divine.

By applying these principles, we avoid seeing and feeling through our masks. This "state of being" can certainly seem disconcerting to some because letting one's interiority run wild is rare, to put it mildly, in any society — *obviously, in some circumstances, professional, societal or familial, the exteriorization must be concealed under a conventional appearance; but it is important to take care not to curb the inner feeling.*

It is this side that we have learned to hide, to bury deep inside us, in order to correspond to the definition of "right-thinking" and the socially correct. The side that children have, opposing someone whom they will embrace the next day, without hate, without resentment, with love. Love of the "Other," of the All, of the Tao, of the Divine, which drives them, carries them, naturally ignites their vitality.

And we, the adults, judge this as inexperience, naivety and immaturity, while it is the common essential Being. Just like them, "I suffer, I love, I reject, all expressed with utter simplicity," thus taking off the stifling mask. This is not a "stage play," but a — *partially* — dissolved ego.

> *Something we also find in:*
> *"When you unclothe yourselves and are not ashamed, and take your garments and lay them beneath your feet like the little children and trample on them, then you will see the Son of the Living One, and you will not be afraid." —Gospel of Thomas 37*

It is this approach that led us to expose what we thought was wrong.

In our writing we intentionally took the opposite of the "spiritually correct," policed and expected. This normalized aspect, you know it, you can read it and hear it continuously.

Now, you must review things and choose the path to take. But, if you do not mind, some advice: *"Forget the gaze of others who, in this area, can only slow you down, if not stop you permanently."*

The biggest difficulty will now be to reject the comfort of thinking and acting as is considered good form, not only by everyone, but also by those thinking they are chosen, different because superior. You may be seen as negative, disillusioned or even odd, but this must be without importance for you. Which will actually be the case.

Make no mistake, we do not reject the established religions and initiatory schools. Christian tradition is respectable, the monasteries contain exceptional beings. Just like Buddhism. The various initiatory teachings have undeniable qualities and shelter in their ranks members who have managed to avoid all pitfalls and thus develop the essence of their tradition.

In every microcosm, one can find the worst, but also the best.

It is true that the essence of these Paths is pure water, untainted, but finding it is extremely difficult, especially for the man living in society.

In the beginning, the "form" is present. It is linked to the different religions, teachings, institutions, groups, etc. It can be appearance, doctrine, tools, rites, and it deliberately makes them stand out.

This "form" is the reference for laymen, but also for apprentices — *even those "experienced"* — who believe themselves initiated only because of their belonging to an organization — *what to think of the fundamentalists?*

We were able to observe the differences that some Knowledgeables thought they saw between prayer, mantra and meditation. Differences stemming from the discursive analysis of the "form," of the superficial, adding to it the products of their culture: historical differences, philosophical contrasts, dissimilarities between religions and between civilizations.

But the more one practices, the more one advances on the Path, the more one realizes that the "forms" are packaging and that they are all derived from a single Tradition, the one present at the origin of man, when the latter was still connected to the Divine, to the Tao, to the Universe — *which we called the primordial Tradition.*

The "forms" differ but the essence remains the same and it can be expressed thusly:

- An "inner thirst" driving the subject on his quest.
- The Reason must silence the Reason so as to awaken the "Other" inside oneself.
- Awareness of the presence of the Soul-breath-Spirit.
- Immanence must lead to transcendence.
- The "divided breath," consciousness / perception, must join the "undivided breath," the Divine, the Tao, the All, for an eternal instant.

Of course, you must research, question, explore, observe, consult, deepen, to finally find the Path that will allow you to access the know-how hidden in the Tools of "The Tradition." Afterwards, you will have to work tirelessly with these tools using the intention of your heart, forgetting any egocentric will, any desire for gain, or to stand out, or to achieve power. And then, one day, one instant, you will let yourself be guided by the "Other" inside you, part of the ineffable, which will allow you to finally drown in the Absolute that you foresee.

This is our wish…

BIBLIOGRAPHY

- The Tanakh
- The Bible
- The Quran
- *The Complete Works of Zhuangzi*, Columbia University Press, 2013
- *Haïkaï de Basho et de ses disciples*, Institut international de coopération intellectuelle, Paris 1936
- Éric Baret, *Yoga*, Édition Almora
- Muriel Baryosher-Chemouny, *La Quête de l'immortalité en Chine*, Édition Dervy
- Charles Baudelaire, *Mon Cœur mis à nu*, Éditions G. Grès et Cie, 1920
- Henri Bergson, *The two sources of morality and religion*, University of Notre-Dame Press, 1977
- Henri Borel, *L'esprit de la Chine*, Édition La main courante
- Henri Borel and Dwight Goddard, *Lao-Tzu's Tao and Wu Wei*, Cosimo Classics
- Michel Chiambretto, *Art et tradition du Travail interne*, Édition Chariot d'or
- Paul Demieville; *T'chan-Zen: Racines et floraisons*, Éditions les deux océans
- Maître Eckhart, *Conseils Spirituels*, Éditions du Relié
- Éric Edelman, *Jésus parlait araméen*
- Bart Ehrman, *Lost Christianities*, Oxford University Press, 2005
- Masaru Emoto, *The Hidden Messages in Water*, Beyond words

publishing, 2004

- Karlfried Graf Dürckheim, *Hara, the vital center of man,* Inner traditions, 2004
- Howard Earl Gardner, *Multiple intelligences, new horizons*, Basic Books, 2006
- Daniel Giraud, *Seng T'san: Hsin Hsin Ming, traité de spiritualité Chan du 6e siècle*, Édition Arfuyen
- C.G. Jung, *Two essays on analytical psychology*, Collected Works, Vol. 7, Princeton University Press, 1967
- C.G. Jung, *Man and his symbols,* Dell Publishing Co., 1968
- C.G. Jung, *Aion: Researches into the Phenomenology of the Self,* Collected Works, vol. 9, Princeton University Press, 1979
- C.G. Jung, *Psychology of the unconscious,* Dover publications, 2003
- Konrad Lorenz, *On Aggression*, Routledge, 2002
- Konrad Lorenz, *Evolution and Modification of Behavior*, The University of Chicago press, 1986
- Konrad Lorenz, *Studies in Human and Animal Behavior*, Harvard University press, 1970
- Konrad Lorenz, *The Foundations of Ethology*, Springer-Verlag New York, 1981
- Paul D. MacLean, *The Triune Brain in Evolution: Role in Paleocerebral Functions,* Plenum, 1990
- Maurice Merleau-Ponty, *Phenomenology of perception,* Routledge, 2012, p. 33
- Yves Moatty, *Kabir: le fils de Ram et d'Allah,* Édition Les deux Océans, 1988
- Hui Neng, *The Platform Sutra of the Sixth Patriarch,* Columbia University Press, 1967
- Pierre Riffard, *Ésotérismes d'ailleurs*, Éditions Robert Laffont, 1997
- Rumi, *Le livre du dedans*, Édition Albin Michel, 1997

- Angélus Silésius, *Dieu est un éternel présent*, Édition Dervy
- John Tauler, *The sermons and conferences of John Tauler*, 1910, p. 280
- Morihei Ueshiba, John Stevens, *The Art of Peace*, Shambhala Publications, 2005, p. 181
- Jean Marc Vivenza, *Le dictionnaire de René Guénon*, Le Mercure Dauphinois, 2002
- Dalai Lama and Sheng Yen, *Meeting of minds*, Dharma Drum Publications, 1999
- Wijrayaratna, *Sermons du Bouddha*, Éditions du Cerf

Bibliography on Taoism

- Lao Tseu, *Tao Te King, Le livre de la Voie et de la Vertu*, Imprimerie Royale, Paris, 1842
- Catherine Despeux, Lao-tseu, *Le guide de l'insondable*, Éditions Entrelacs, 2010
- *Le Lao-Tseu, suivi des quatre canons de l'empereur jaune*, trad. Jen Lévy, Albin Michel, 2009
- *Tao Te King*, Albin Michel, 1984
- Liou Kia-Hway et Benedykt Grynpas, *Philosophes taoïstes*, Bibliothèque de la Pléiade
- *TAO TÖ KING Le livre de la voie et de la vertu*, nouvelle traduction de Conradin Von Lauer, Éditions Jean de Bonnot, 1990
- *Tao Te King*, trad. Claude Larre, Les Carnets, 2008
- *Tao Te King*, trad. Stephen Mitchell

Bibliography on Kabir

- *Kabir le fils de Ram et d'Allah*, Yves Moatty, Les deux océans, 2000
- *Au cabaret de l'amour: Paroles de Kabîr*, Charlotte Vaudeville, Gallimard,1986

- *Kabir: Une expérience mystique au-delà des religions,* Michel Guay, Albin Michel, 2012
- *La Flûte de l'Infini / Poèmes Kabir,* André Gide, Henriette Mirabaud-Thorens — traduction — suivi du recueil intégral des Poèmes, Gallimard, 2012
- *Cent huit perles, anthologie de poèmes de Kabir,* Les deux océans, 1995

Bibliography on the Gospel of Thomas

- *L'évangile de Thomas,* Jean Yves Leloup, Albin Michel, 1986
- *L'évangile selon Thomas,* A. Guillaumont, H.C. Puech Collège de France, Paris, 1959
- *Évangile selon Thomas,* É. Gillabert, P. Bourgeois, Y. Haas, Collection Metanoia, 1979

www.ingramcontent.com/pod-product-compliance
Lightning Source LLC
Chambersburg PA
CBHW010859090426
42738CB00018B/3443